ARTIVISM

THE BATTLE FOR MUSEUMS IN THE ERA OF POSTMODERNISM

Alexander Adams

Foreword by
Michael Sandle

Illustrated by the author

SOCIETAS
essays in political
& cultural criticism

imprint-academic.com

Copyright © Alexander Adams, 2022

The moral rights of the author have been asserted.
No part of this publication may be reproduced in any form
without permission, except for the quotation of brief passages
in criticism and discussion.

Published in the UK by
Imprint Academic Ltd., PO Box 200, Exeter EX5 5YX, UK

Distributed in the USA by
Ingram Book Company,
One Ingram Blvd., La Vergne, TN 37086, USA

ISBN 9781788360739 paperback

A CIP catalogue record for this book is available from the
British Library and US Library of Congress

By the same author

Verse

Three Strikes (2011)
Seahorse (2013)
The Crows of Berlin (2013)
On Dead Mountain (2015)
On Art (2018)
On Art II (2020)

Fiction

Letter About Spain (2016)
Berlin, October (2016)
London, Winter (2017)
Selima in the Orchard (2018)

Art

Works on Paper (2004)
Noctes (2005)
Icarus (2005)
Ruins and Landscapes (2007)
Paintings on Paper (2008)
New Gouaches (2010)
Portraiture (2013)
Nouvelles Peintures (2018)

Criticism

Culture War: Art, Identity Politics and Cultural Entryism (2019)
Iconoclasm, Identity Politics and the Erasure of History (2020)
Edgar Degas (2022)
René Magritte (2022)

Contents

Foreword *by Michael Sandle*	vii
Introduction	ix
Case Study: Cultural Entryism at the ICA	1
1. Art, Politics and Political Art	8
Case Study: Artivism Against Nazism	31
2. State Art and Utilitarianism	36
Case Study: Banksy, Cosy Artivist	59
3. The Managerial Elite and Artivism	66
Case Study: Extinction Rebellion, Handmaiden of Technocracy	80
4. Institutions and Artivism	86
Case Study: Stuckists as Anti-Artivists	98
5. The Business of Artivism	104
Case Study: Artivism for Migration	129
6. The Psychology of Artivism	135
Case Study: North African Artivism	141
7. Resisting Artivism	147
Conclusions	152

Appendices

A:	Correspondence between the author and ICA, 2018	156
B:	ICA political campaigning, 2020	162
C:	ICA press releases, 2020	166
D:	Letter to the Charities Commission of England, 2021	172

About the Authors   174

Textual History   175

Acknowledgements   175

Bibliography   176

Endnotes   181

Michael Sandle

Foreword

Alexander Adams has written an extremely timely book and I am very pleased that I have been asked to write the foreword for it. I became first aware of Alexander Adams at a webinar organised by the Public Statues and Sculpture Association, of which I am currently the Patron. The webinar was about the fashion for toppling statues in the present climate of historical—or maybe that should read "hysterical"—revisionism. I noticed that many of the non-speaking participants wanted the moderator to stop him saying his piece because they did not—amongst other things—want to hear themselves described as "the Managerial Class", which in many cases they were. I don't think there were many forklift drivers present. Adams will make more enemies with this, his third book, because he always has had the moral courage to say exactly what he thinks in the present culture of real or perceived politically correct and woke issues, which often savagely repress any contrary view.

    I am happy to praise *Artivism: The Battle for Museums in the Era of Postmodernism* for several reasons. We live in dangerous and, I believe, decadent times when freedom of speech and opinion is under threat and language is being constantly traduced from its real meaning. Adams uses language consistently correctly because he is exceptionally erudite and his research is far reaching and scholarly—no tortured or incomprehensible sentences, thank God! His arguments are laid down with exemplary clarity throughout this book. You do not to have to accept every one of his views but he relentlessly hones in on to his main target — "artivism" — with ice-cold precision. He doesn't take prisoners.

All "artivism" is not necessarily bad. In this book there is a very moving account of two women artists — Claude Cahun and Suzanne Malherbe, who during the 1930s were both involved in Surrealist and anti-fascism movements. The latter they were able to physically act out during the Nazi occupation of Jersey, at great risk to themselves, and were in fact sentenced to death; fortunately, as the war was drawing to a close, it wasn't carried out. But — and this is the point that the author makes so abundantly clear — much of "artivism" is indeed malevolent. The so-called "deep state" is often involved and if anyone thinks that is just a conspiracy theory, they will have forgotten the CIA and MI6 infiltration of *Encounter* magazine. If anyone thinks that the notion of the deep state is just a fantasy, they should look up Operation Gladio.

It is a melancholy fact that "real" (or what could be described as "high") art is under threat by "artivism", for reasons which Adams is able to lay bare with forensic accuracy. The current art world is more corrupt than ever, with museums and actors like the Frieze Fair acting as "tastemakers" and exercising far too much control. Our once great institutions bear some responsibility for this malaise, as Adams points out beyond controversy. I am possibly not free from bias when I write that this book hits very many nails firmly on the head, because I now have the mindset of a taxi driver — no disparagement meant to taxi drivers — but when I look at so much of contemporary art now, I can't help thinking: "Do you call this rubbish art? My two-year-old daughter could do better!" I mean it too. Art today has become an inflated and politicised industry instead of the vocation it was when I started my career. As Winston Churchill could have said: "Never, in the history of Western civilisation, has so little art been achieved by so many!"

Michael Sandle, October 2021

Introduction

In our opinion there's nothing more dangerous or necessary today than an artivist, or whatever we decide to call them.
— Arcadi Poch & Daniela Poch[1]

Who today has greater capacity to shock, inspire and provoke than the artist-as-activist?

The artivist can operate in back streets or command space in museums. He can coordinate an event worldwide or operate alone. At his word, a thousand people gather and disrobe; he can wrap a landmark building in fabric. His name appears in the press and social media, yet you would not recognise him if he walked past you. He is a prankster. He subverts unobtrusively but also gatecrashes press conferences, fakes suicide, stages orgies. He mocks religion and burns the national flag. More than a rebel, he is a holy man. He can fight for the marginalised, highlight injustice, embarrass governments. He can make people think; he can make them weep. He can feed the hungry and reverse pollution. He is a force for good in the world, someone who holds the great to account. He combines the archetypes of intellectual, rock star and political prisoner.

All art is political. Well, all art has a political aspect in its production, consumption and discussion. So does buying an apple. Where one buys that apple, whether one boycotts a type of apple due to its country of origin, whether one buys in person or shops online, whether one pays in cash or by card, whether one uses a store card (selling one's consumption data in return for a discount) and why one buys an apple rather than growing it — answers to these questions reflect a complex socio-political economy. Art (like all action) can be political on many levels.

There will be criticism that the argument of this book — the first book broadly negative about the implications and practice of the phenomenon of activism-as-art — that it rests upon the naïve argument that "art should not be political" or that "curators should be unbiased". It will be set out clearly in this book that, while there is no true neutrality in curation of art or in distribution of resources by arts organisations, neutrality within publicly-owned/funded venues is a goal for which it is worth striving. Artists should be free to do what they will but it is not incumbent upon any public body to host that art.

Artivism has two common meanings: (a) fine art that is intended to effect political/social change, and (b) political action that is described as fine art, again intended to effect political change. In this book, my focus will be on the latter definition. This book examines how artivism has developed as an outgrowth of both political art and social protest. We look at the meta-politics of artivism. Who has a vested interest in the consumption of art resources by artivists? Why is activism-as-art such an effective tool for influencing society? We encounter evidence of the webs of mutual exploitation of socio-political movements by artists, administrators and patrons (and vice versa) that underpin the artivist economy. As set out throughout this book, the Faustian pact that arts administrators have made (in order to gain fleeting relevance and signal their values) has the potential to destroy the public-arts funding model. Case studies of notable examples and aspects of artivism are interspersed between chapters. Documentary material is printed in Appendices. For anyone wishing to oppose political programming in public art venues, these documents may provide useful starting references.

Although this book is written with a concentration on Great Britain, I (regretfully) use the Americanism "art museum" (instead of British "art gallery") to avoid confusion, especially in an edition to be read internationally. There needed to be easy distinction between the public tax-funded art gallery and private commercial art gallery. (Privately owned non-tax-funded art museums arise only rarely in this book.) "Art museum" means public tax-funded art gallery; "art gallery" refers a private commercial gallery; "art venue" refers to any public building that displays art or multiple art forms; "the public arts" means state-supported arts. This is not ideal but it avoids tiresome repetition of definitions. Within quotes, emphases are preserved from the original texts.

October 2021

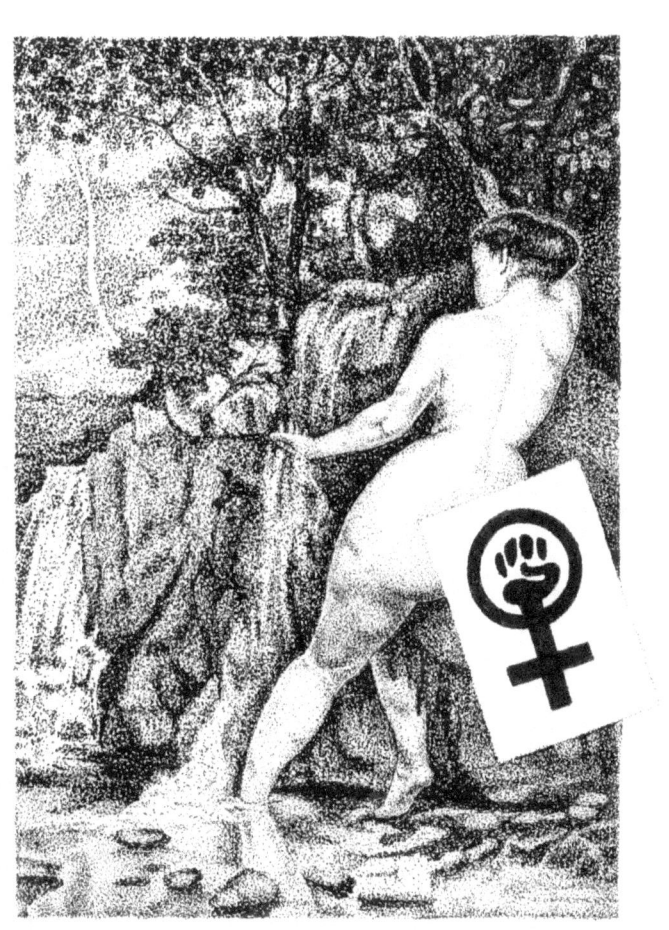

Case Study

Cultural Entryism at the ICA

On 1 October 2018, the Institute of Contemporary Arts, London, hosted a celebratory dinner and interview for Chelsea Manning. Manning is a political activist and commentator on issues such as intelligence gathering, surveillance methods and transgender issues. The event included a dialogue on these topics and questions from the mainstream press, which heavily covered the occasion. Manning has no expertise on art and the dinner was unrelated to any display at the ICA. It seemed as though the ICA was expressing solidarity with a social campaigner rather than fulfilling any cultural function.[2]

The ICA, established as a venue for advanced art in 1947, had made its name as one of the few venues that exhibited difficult art in the immediate post-war period. It had staged a number of seminal displays and events, particularly of Francis Bacon (1955), Richard Hamilton's *Man, Machine and Motion* (1955), the Independent Group and J.G. Ballard's *Crash!* (1968). It was known for its film programme and a bookshop that stocked rare art-related publications. By the late 1990s, the ICA was struggling for relevance in a London full of venues for contemporary art, film and books. It drifted to the fringe, embracing increasingly niche performances and talks, often with a political slant. Currently, the ICA receives funding from the Department for Digital, Culture, Media and Sport (DCMS) via the Arts Council of England (ACE) and the British Council. In 2020, the ICA received £789,000 from the government's Culture Recovery Fund, taking its annual income from taxes to over £1.5m.

On 16 January 2020, the ICA issued a press release in which it stated that it had permitted exhibiting American artivist Cameron Rowland to issue (on behalf of the ICA) a mortgage on five doors of the ICA, at £1,000 per door. (These doors are made of mahogany and Rowland's press release linked sourcing of mahogany to historical slavery.) The ICA does not own the property but leases it from the Crown Estate. The knowing issuance of an invalid legal contract was done to make a political statement.[3]

During the government-imposed Covid-19 lockdown, beginning in March 2020, the ICA was forced to close its doors. In place of its usual programme, it issued daily press releases written by ICA curators, the director and invited curators, distributed on the website and via emails. These contained recommendations for cultural material, such as films, documentaries, poems, music, books, recorded lectures and websites. While there were recommendations for artistic material, many recommendations were primarily or wholly political. Recurrent topics were support for the Black Lives Matter protests, LGBTQ activism, trans-activism, eco-activism, sex workers, migrants, also campaigning against capitalism, policing, incarceration and the legacy of historical slavery. A press release on 2 June 2020 displays the Antifa symbol and linked to an argument for defunding the police.[4] It recommended a book called *Why I Stopped Talking to White People About Race* and promoted a fundraiser. "This online fundraiser hosted by Ignota Books is set up to raise money for Black liberation organisations and bail funds in support of resistance movements in the US […]"[5] In another press release, a Muslim artivist wrote an invective against the "openly islamophobic, Hindu nationalist government" in Kashmir.[6] The ICA hosted pro-Islamic content but did not do so for Christian content.[7]

The ICA had given itself over to a platform that included every leftist cause (ranging from gibes at President Trump to offering apparent support for extremist political groups) and using arts funds for non-charitable purposes. On 31 January 2020, it had hosted a "Queer techno rave INFERNO take over [of] the ICA's Theatre, Bar and Cinema with an all-night programme of music, queer porn and performance art".[8] A clear provocation, this also had minimal art content. How did the ICA's search for relevance lead the once-premier art venue to a series of aggressive stunts and violations of standards expected of a public art gallery, one situated on the Mall, within sight of Buckingham Palace, and supported by ACE?

Director of the ICA

The trajectory of the ICA in recent years is understandable if we look at the career of its director, Stefan Kalmar. Mr Kalmar is a German curator and arts administrator. He studied at University of Hildesheim, Germany, and then went on to Goldsmiths College, London, for a qualification in Cultural and Curatorial Studies. He held senior positions at Cubitt Gallery (London), Institute of Visual Culture (Cambridge), Kunstverein München (Munich) and Artists Space (New York). He was a curator for an event in France and was on the judging panel of the Turner Prize in 2014. He was appointed director of the ICA in 2016.

In 2020, the director described his route to London:

> Four years ago, while camping out at a friend's place in Brooklyn, I woke up in disbelief to the 2016 US election results. Later that morning I met members of the MTL+ Collective at Artists Space Books & Talks. I'll never forget sitting in a circle with them, a circle that grew bigger and bigger during the course of the morning—as did the tears, the angst and the pain, as people talked about their fears of deportation and potentially losing life-saving healthcare. Both the last four years and the past 72 hours have shown us that such fears have become part of our daily reality, but we must never let

them become our normality. I booked my flight to London to join the Institute of Contemporary Arts exactly four years ago.[9]

When he took charge at the ICA, he set about accelerating the organisation's progressive agenda. "Education for all, healthcare for all, university for all, pensions for all, universal basic incomes for all, culture for all. For the ICA and for me, these are not just some crazy ideas."[10] Mr Kalmar claimed government austerity threatened the public sector and stated that public arts needed 50% funding from taxation (he gives the ICA's public income as comprising 21% of its budget). He suggested that his organisation deserved special protection, yet made no commitment to represent the views of the majority of the British population.

Following the illegal toppling, defacing and drowning of the statue of Edward Colston MP by a mob in Bristol on 7 June 2020,[11] Mr Kalmar celebrated it with a press release: "Not only do they all need to go, but when will we be willing to address reparation payments to all those who were forced into slavery, and to their families living here today?"[12] Not only did a foreign director of a tax-funded arts body approve of the liquidation of cultural heritage, he demanded more of it. He did so not as a private person but in his official capacity and through the ICA press office.

I have no animosity — indeed, no feelings at all — towards Mr Kalmar. He is a component of a politically progressive elite, floating between venues in a global network of state/charity-supported contemporary art venues and events. Detached and insulated, this elite consists of what author David Goodhart describes as "anywheres" — individuals who have no strong attachment to place, people or national history and view themselves as internationalists and world citizens — in contrast to the "somewheres", who have a firm attachment to regional community and locale.[13] There is nothing to distinguish Mr Kalmar from the curatorial-administrative caste of anywheres who staff state-art venues worldwide.

Elitism and corruption

Following the Manning event, I contacted the ICA, the Charities Commission of England (CCE) (as regulator of the ICA, as a Registered Charity) and Jeremy Wright MP (as Minister of State for DCMS), in charge of oversight for the ICA and ACE (ICA's largest funder). I outlined that the ICA had acted contrary to its founding document and CCE regulations barring Registered Charities from political campaigning outside of its core purpose, as it seemed that the Manning event was not artistic programming and was effectively political campaigning by proxy. Additionally, it seemed that the ICA had diverted funding from provision of arts to political campaigning, an act that was at least unethical and possibly illegal.

I received notification from DCMS and CCE that my objection had been received but no announcement was made about any resultant investigation. No sanction was imposed on the ICA. A subsequent submission of evidence by me to the House of Commons Digital, Culture, Media and Sport Committee on 9 March 2020 regarding the apparent inaction of the CCE to reprimand the ICA likewise led to no action. Mr Kalmar's reply to my initial letter[14] responded that notable speakers had been hosted by the ICA previously and that the Manning event was no different. Non-art activities were permitted if they were on topics of interest to artists—a defence that meant any speaker could address any subject, regardless of connection (or lack of one) to art. I described that response as the "definition of both elitism and corruption".

On 7 July 2021, the ICA reopened its doors after Covid-19 lockdown by launching a display called *War Inna Babylon: The Community's Struggle For Truths and Rights*, "curated by London-based racial advocacy and community organisation, Tottenham Rights, and independent curators Kamara Scott and Rianna Jade Parker".[15] According to the ICA, the display consisted of documentary material relating to black community–police relations in London, comprising "tributes from victims' families" and "film screenings, community educational groups, talks, cultural events, performances, and a digital presentation focusing on the interrelation between artificial intelligence (AI) and racism".[16] (One of the contributors was the collective Forensic Architecture, discussed later.) No art was mentioned in the press release. Whatever the merits of arguments relating to this serious issue, the presented material did not belong in a public art venue.

Once again, objections were raised.[17] When a national newspaper approached DCMS, the minister failed to condemn the apparent impropriety.[18] As I wrote to the journalist who wrote that article: "If the ICA is permitted to use the 'contextualisation' argument, then it is freed of all restraints and can engage in any non-art activity. In that case, our public art venues are living on borrowed time before they fall to political activism. The ICA is making a mockery of company regulation, public funding and charity status, knowing that it will not be held to account by timid authorities." The ICA's contextualisation defence covers any social issue, which can be used as carte blanche to open its doors to campaigners who can present propaganda and non-art material unchallenged in the venue. The aim of using art to instigate directed social change has been implemented without altering its founding charter or terms of any grant. This is a prime example of cultural entryism in the high-culture sector.[19]

Consequences

On 10 August 2021, the announcement came that Mr Kalmar was resigning: "[…] the moment now feels right for me to hand over to the next generation to lead this iconic institution with care, compassion and vision."[20] He added that "what's happening in the UK is worrying. The historic arm's-length principle between the government and cultural institutions that it directly funds… [is] being undermined."[21] Mr Kalmar sought to highlight supposed interference by politicians in artistic matters. What had actually happened was that the ICA had been caught out apparently diverting art funds into politics and that the ICA had interpreted the threat or expectation of reprimand as political interference. The threat of the enforcement of regulations had damaged Mr Kalmar's credibility and imperilled the ICA's funding.

From one perspective, this looks like a victory for reactionaries or the establishment over artivism. However, as we shall see, artivism and the establishment are intimately linked. A more plausible analysis is that Mr Kalmar and top staff at the ICA had miscalculated how far they could push the envelope. Having put out political content for about three years, the *War Inna Babylon* display was simply too blatant to go unignored. That does not suggest the establishment disagrees with community-centred policing or racial-bias training for law enforcement (two subjects touched on in the display), just that this display breached etiquette. The optics were wrong. The departure of Mr Kalmar does not imply that DCMS, ACE or CCE disagrees with artivist programming. In January 2022, the Turkish curator-administrator Bengi Ünsal was announced as the next director of the ICA. Press releases described her as "the first woman to serve as the organization's director in 55 years".

The ICA provides an ideal case study for capture of long-standing art organisations by activists — or at least by administrators and curators who believe their social commitments and group affiliations take precedence over any duties towards institution, public and the integrity of art. Just because an organisation has a long and distinguished history, the principles and protocols of that period of success are not necessarily perpetuated unless they are both written into its constitution and upheld by the staff. Study of documents in the Appendices will show that top staff at the ICA did not have to change a word in its Memorandum of Association before subverting the organisation's purpose. If bodies charged with overseeing organisations (regulating agencies, funders, partners and mainstream and specialist press) are sympathetic towards the goals of activists within an art organisation, then gross deviations of function and ethos can be achieved with ease.

One

Art, Politics & Political Art

All human action has political ramifications; art cannot be treated excluding politics. However, the greater part of fine art (whether or not it is directed towards instrumentalist ends) has many other levels of consideration which are more important than politics. Fields of the aesthetic, allegorical, narrative, iconographic, biographical, documentary, historical and technical assessment—inasmuch as they stand apart from politics—are of greater importance than the political reading for the purposes of evaluation and interpretation of the majority of fine art in the Western tradition. That said, the following outline includes instances of overt socio-political messaging within art over the ages. Some examples of what we might now call artivism are included to show how artivism has deep roots in the twentieth century.

From ancient Greece to revolutionary France

The Parthenon (447–438 BC) on the Acropolis was financed using the tributes of member regions of the Delian League (or Athenian Empire). As such, the temple was at least in part a departure from existing religious architecture devoted to the glory of the god, in that the Parthenon was also a tribute to the power of the state—a state which extended its military and diplomatic protection to neighbouring *poleis*. It was a political statement by the *polis* of

Athens regarding its power and status, as well its artistry, and was occasioned by the Athenian leadership of the Greek alliance which defeated the invading Persian Empire. (We derive the word "politics" from the Greek *politiká* (affairs of cities).) There is debate as to the religious importance of the Parthenon, which was not specifically host to the cult of Athena Polias, and may have functioned as a state treasury. That aside, we can see the Parthenon as a political statement.

Art has a role in diplomatic soft power. Starting in the late medieval period, paintings and tapestries were commissioned by the nobility to celebrate military victories, dynastic marriages and foreign conquests, and by the Church to reinforce theological doctrine. Art was displayed to impress ambassadors and given as gifts to foreign powers. Marxist historians point out that art displays class privilege by virtue of the material resources necessary to commission it; it was a message absorbed subliminally by low-class individuals, who would encounter such rare and costly products infrequently, mainly in churches. At a very basic level, coinage of the day displayed the profile of the ruler. It was reserved to the ruler the right to mint coins as legal tender. Image-making on a scale that was grand or ubiquitous was the privilege of ruler and Church.

Courtly spectacles of the Renaissance—festivals held to mark dynastic and civic occasions, rather than the usual saints' days— included elaborate performances and curiosities, which called upon the skills and inventions of courtiers. Michelangelo made a snow figure for Piero de Medici; Leonardo da Vinci devised a walking mechanical lion for Francis I in 1515. Other artists and craftsmen made ingenious ephemeral devices and settings for court masques. Although the main purpose was to amuse and entertain the court, a secondary purpose was to enact conspicuous consumption. Such expensive and short-lived extravaganzas were a show of power and wealth, precisely because they were simultaneously wonderful and wasteful. When we consider the spectacles of artivism today, it is worth viewing them similarly. Spending large sums on a temporary spectacle ostensibly highlighting environmental perils is not just a means of promoting the message but a material manifestation of the power of commissioning bodies, wealth of donors, prestige of the artist (always credited, never anonymous) and social status of super-rich global-elite attendees participating in the event premier. Large-scale art performance and installation are power politics; the willingness of the powerful to impose a statement upon a locale and resident population is in itself a display of domination. In the case of environmental alarmism, it is a message of ideological hegemony, for no dissent on that issue is entertained by the art-world elite. Many contemporary artists promoted by the media, by public arts and by subsidised art presses are entirely supported by grants, prizes, stipends and public commissions; they have no support among connoisseurs or public.

All revolutionaries take up the standards of bygone eras as they displace the then dominant one. "Even a people advertising their iconoclasm use, through necessity, both the visual props and the language of orthodoxy."[22] When the thinkers of the French Republicans sought to replace symbols of the *Ancien Régime*, they modelled their French Republic on the Roman Republic. They carved busts that echoed ancient marbles and styled themselves on politicians of the Senate. Jacques-Louis David, a prominent revolutionary and member of the National Assembly (as well as the most distinguished painter of his generation), was called upon to arrange festivals and funerals for the state. These events expressed the political intentions of the state, fusing national symbols, ancient references and utopian philosophy derived from Rousseau. David was deputised to design a celebration mounted by the state in central Paris on Bastille Day, 1793, including a bonfire of regalia and a parade before a giant statue of Hercules.[23]

We could call these the true origins of artivism: state-funded spectacles that were impermanent and intended to be participated in by the populace in a mystical ceremony of grandeur, novel contrivance, assertion of political will and shared symbolic narrative.

There is more than a touch of the religious rite about artivism. The artivist-shaman-priestess proscribes the place and time of communion, her assistants prepare the space and provide necessary materials. The tribe gathers to attend the publicly-announced rite, respectfully assisting by witnessing and participating as directed. The Actionist event may include shedding of blood; the feminist performance may involve nudity. Attendees are moved to tears or reduced to silence. The tribal bond is reaffirmed through observance, acts of charity and communal activity under the guidance of the artivist-shaman-priestess. If art museums are secular cathedrals of a post-religious age, then the artivist or performance artist is their priestess. Like every priestess, after serving as novitiate she is awarded a title, given due respect, accredited with unique attributes and paid for performing rites. The great painters are venerated saints—who suffered physically and emotionally to do their good works, accounts of whom we scour for spiritual instruction, whose paintings are relics which the devote endure pilgrimages to worship—but it is the living artivist who acts as link between congregation and the spirit of art.

From Romanticism to social realism

Romanticism allowed artists greater range of expressiveness in their pursuit of moral and social persuasion. Francisco Goya's images of war were, if not a cry for passivism, a call for pity and restraint. Théodore Géricault (1791–1824) painted amputated body parts and the corpses of executed criminals, partly to research the processes of decay and dismemberment for his *The Raft of 'La Méduse'* (1819). He drew the hanging of a man, which he witnessed on a stay in London. He was opposed to the death penalty and wanted to present the horror of deliberate judicial killing. His portraits of mental-asylum inmates indicate great empathy with outcasts and unfortunates, partly due to the artist's alleged depressive episodes and from humanitarian advocacy.

Like his hero Géricault, Belgian Romantic proto-Symbolist Antoine Wiertz (1806–1865) was an ardent opponent of capital punishment. He depicted executions by guillotine, fascinated and horrified. Like many idealistic reformers of his era, he condemned Napoleon's militarism and authoritarianism and highlighted social issues. *The Premature Burial* (1854) has a terrified man breaking out of a coffin, stamped *Mort du cholera*. (Cholera produces a coma state in victims (casually indistinguishable from death) and during outbreaks living victims were sometimes hastily interred whilst in this condition.) He advocated childcare to prevent neglect and death of infants while their mothers were working. He also depicted (in a sensation manner) cannibalism due to starvation. It is fair to conclude that the deeply-conflicted Wiertz was a passionate social reformer, not least to atone for his ingrained morbidness, which caused him alternating pleasure and shame.[24]

Eugène Delacroix (1798–1863) became celebrated for his political paintings. These broadcast the suffering of Christian Greeks under the Ottoman yoke (*Massacre at Chios* (1824), *Greece on the Ruins of the Missolonghi* (1826)) and the republican toppling of the Bourbon monarchy (*Liberty Leading the People* (1830)). His depictions of France's newly acquired possession of Algeria had an underlying Orientalist-colonialist purpose. Delacroix himself had a naturally aristocratic temperament sympathetic towards heroism rather than reform; he tended to see his age as one of decline. His attachment to art of the past—especially the religious paintings of Rubens—is a true reflection of his reactionary character. His painting *The Natchez* (1835), showing a Native American couple, is evidence of a yearning for the authenticity found in ancient tribal and familial bonds—in opposition to the progressive Whig view of history, with its narrative of inevitable development towards a secular, non-national, industrialised, scientific future.

Jean-François Millet (1814–1875) painted peasants in a way that was dramatic and immediate. The lot of the peasantry was an issue that divided liberals from traditionalists and royalists. The nascent socialist movement in France (including Saint-Simonianism) put the plight of the peasantry at the centre of its case. Millet's *The Gleaners* (1857) met a hostile reception when exhibited at the Paris Salon. In the painting, peasant women are engaged in the back-breaking labour of picking individual grains from the recently harvested field. The grain of the harvest was owned by the landlord but loose grain was permitted to peasants. Showing hard labour of working women as a remnant of seigneury was considered contentious by urban bourgeois salon-attendees. Gustave Courbet's contemporaneous paintings of labourers betray a similar communitarian outlook, one that became manifest during Courbet's participation in the revolutionary Paris Commune.

The Victorian period was the heyday of narrative art performing moral instruction and social consciousness-raising. As well as depicting inspiring virtuous acts, painters, printmakers and illustrators addressed social issues in celebrated art. Driven to prick the consciences of viewers or agitate for reform, these pictures—in addition to the vast number of didactic prints in books, journals and progressive newspapers—highlighted social issues to be addressed or overcome through charity, legislation or increased understanding and tolerance. The themes of this art included rural poverty (Ilya Repin, *Barge Haulers on the Volga* (1870–3)), urban poverty (Thomas Benjamin Kennington, *The Pinch of Poverty* (1891)), incarceration (Gustave Doré, *Prisoners' Round* (1872)), emigration (Ford Madox Brown, *The Last of England* (1855)), marital infidelity (Augustus Egg, *Past and Present* (1858)), extra-marital sex (William Holman Hunt, *The Awakening Conscience* (1853)), illegitimacy (Madox Brown, *Take Your Son, Sir!* (1856–7)), alcoholism (George Cruikshank, *The Bottle* suite (1847)), conflict trauma (Lady Butler, *Calling the Roll After an Engagement, Crimea* (1874)), homelessness (Luke Fildes, *Applicants to a Casual Ward* (1869)), orphanhood (Frank Holl, *Deserted – A Foundling* (1874)), prostitution (Dante Gabriel Rossetti, *Found* (1854–81)), public sanitation (W.A. Atkinson, *The First Public Drinking Fountain* (1859–60)), tuberculosis (Cristóbal Rojas, *First and Last Communion* (1888)), syphilis (Félicien Rops, *Mors Syphilitica* (c. 1880)), lower-class suicide (G.F. Watts, *Found Drowned* (c. 1850)), rural eviction (Butler, *Evicted* (1889–90)), itinerant labour (Hubert von Herkomer, *Hard Times* (1885)), fishermen's death at sea (Frank Bramley, *A Hopeless Dawn* (1888)), gambling (Robert Braithwaite Martineau, *The Last Day in the Old Home* (1862)), bankruptcy (Vladimir Makovsky, *Bankruptcy* (1881)), industrial labour disputes (Herkomer, *On Strike* (c. 1891)) and the situation of women artists (Emily Mary Osborn, *Nameless and Friendless* (1857)). All of these pictures have artistic merit and have considerable skill in conveying the creators' social messages.

Socialist Realism versus Surrealism

Early Soviet art was infused with the extreme idealism of religion and the aggression of revolution. Vladimir Mayakovsky's Futurist manifesto of 1918 announced, "the old regime rested on three foundations: political slavery, social slavery, spiritual slavery."[25] It called for artists (as workers) to be handed the means of production and ended by demanding requisitioning of foodstuffs for the people of Russia. In the early Soviet period, artists were set to the making of pictures, murals, sculpture, theatre sets, posters, fabrics, clothing, furniture, crockery, buildings and every material component of a new world fit for Soviet Man.[26] There were to be no restrictions on what artists should be able to do to serve fellow citizens. With limitless ambition, blurring of boundaries between fields and without recognition of any such being as a private person, early Soviet art set the template for the political zealotry of artivism in later periods.

The realpolitik of socialism in a single country under Stalin curbed the excesses of this heady period. The risk of alienating an artistically conservative population with radical modernism, ceaseless intellectual vanguardism and waste of resources were identified as contrary to the needs of the state. A rapid reversal led to Modernist art being consigned to museum basements or destroyed, with artists being directed to produce realistic art. Andrei Zhadanov set out the official line in Stalin's USSR regarding the arts in 1932:

[...] the truthfulness and historical concreteness of the artistic portrayal should be combined with the ideological remoulding and education of the toiling people in the spirit of socialism. This method in *belles lettres* and literary criticism is what we call the method of socialist realism. [...] one cannot be an engineer of human souls without knowing the technique of literary work [...] You have many types of weapons. Soviet literature has every opportunity of employing these types of weapons (genres, styles, forms and methods of literary creation) in their diversity and fullness, selecting all the best that has been created in this sphere by all previous epochs.[27]

This was literature (and all the arts) set to the purpose of being utile for the people, guided by the state as representative of the people.

Under the guiding principles of Socialist Realism—essentially, "realism" (i.e. conformity to Party doctrine), legibility, lack of ambiguity and freedom from bourgeois formalism—artists produced images of an ideal reality. Socialist Realism is inhabited by attentive schoolchildren, beneficent leaders, contented peasants, devoted soldiers and workers united in fraternal labour. Socialist Realism did not dictate a style beyond adherence to figuration, be that naturalism, Impressionism or restrained Expressionism. Artists were permitted a degree of freedom within the constraints of the Artists Union (founded, significantly, in 1932) and political conformity. There was no such entity as a private person in the USSR.

This approach held largely true for artists within Nazi Germany and its occupied territories, from 1933 to 1945. The pressure to produce what was naturalistic or traditional in style was greater than in the USSR, although conversely there was less emphasis on political content. Art that was traditional in genre, conservative in style and (crucially) not deemed anti-German in content was suitable for exhibition and publication, and for acquisition by public bodies. The state in Nazi Germany was less important in terms of commissioning and vetting art than it was in the USSR, although artist-union membership was advantageous for German artists. While the USSR was concerned to produce political art useful to the state, the Nazis were concerned to produce non-political art that did not oppose the state, though as a matter of distinction, official art produced in both countries was largely conventional, anodyne, technically competent and thematically unambiguous. It can be almost impossible to distinguish examples from the two states.

In Italy under Fascism, a wide range of styles was tolerated and even met with official approval. Traditional art, Art Deco, Futurism and Expressionism and more experimental hybrids of figuration (Novecento, Metaphysical Art) flourished. Elements of patriotism, conservatism, modernism, Catholic revival, militarism and historicism appeared in the art but were by no means required, except when commissioned for an official purpose. The sole stipulation was absence of anti-Fascist or unpatriotic content; this naturally entailed suppression of pro-communist art. In this respect, Fascist Italy was both a controlled environment and significantly more vibrant and artistically plural than Nazi Germany and the USSR.

In the 1920s and 1930s, the Mexican Muralist movement was led by José Clemente Orozco (1883–1949), Diego Rivera (1886–1957) and David Alfaro Siqueiros (1896–1974). They were committed to communism and benefited from the patronage of the post-Revolutionary socialist government. Commissioned to decorate major public buildings, they created art that reflected the history of Mexico, the life of people (with attention paid to the indigenous peoples) and Marxist politics, incorporating the art and customs of Mexico with touches of modernism, as found in the paintings of Picasso and Fernand Léger. It was an attempt to distinguish Mexico from both the USA and Europe, in an art intended to reach the masses. It was notable for its patriotism, social consciousness and dependence on public funds. Generally, the quality was high, with muralists finding suitable balances between narrative and formal demands of large flat surfaces in irregular shapes. Execution required teams of technicians and assistant painters, turning art for the masses into art made by workshop teams.

Pablo Picasso (1881–1973) joined the Partie communiste français (PCF) upon the liberation of Paris in 1944. This was an expression of commitment to humanitarianism and anti-war sentiment, in addition to recognising the part played by communists in the French Resistance. This complements the sympathy for the poor found in the Blue and Rose periods. During the Spanish Civil War, Picasso supported the Republicans and produced a satirical anti-Franco print. His *Guernica* (1937) combined political protest with ancient symbolism and autobiographical associations in a painting made for display in the Spanish pavilion, organised by the Republican government, at the 1937 Paris International Exposition. In the post-war period, Picasso allowed his art to be used for PCF causes (including peace-conference posters). He lent his imprimatur to communism, which struggled against the characterisation of Socialist Realism stifling artistic expression. Picasso realised his stature was being deployed to add lustre and credibility to international socialism; he was content that the cause advanced social reform and opposed the re-emergence of fascism. Like artists such as Frida Kahlo, René Magritte and others, Picasso did not have a commitment to workers seizing the means of production nor to a state led by members of the proletariat as a step towards a world unified in a final stage of super-abundance of goods. Picasso's utopian visions of the 1940s and 1950s are reversions to an arcadian prehistory rather than an expression of belief in a future utopia of New Man and any Wellsian single world government.

From the mid-1920s to the 1940s, the Surrealists struggled with their pledged loyalty to the PCF, which caused schisms in the movement. The artivism of the Surrealists was the intrusion into everyday life of interventions which upset expectations. This included acts of anarchic poetry and ones of violent anti-clericalism (such as kicking a priest in the street). Leader André Breton advocated random violence.[28] The Surrealists supported political assassination[29] and patricide.[30] The justification for acts of revolt such as these was to bring about a psychic revolution to complement the social revolution of communism. Liberation from received perception was the goal of Surrealism and breaking boundaries between life, art and political action was originally a Surrealist strategy, inspiring later performance art, Happenings, conceptual art and artivism.

Salvador Dalí (1904–1989) was originally a supporter of communism and anarchism; his commitment to these soon ended but the affinity with provocative positions was a lifelong tendency. Dalí was expelled from the Surrealist movement due to his paintings that depicted Lenin in ways that were ambiguous or disrespectful (in *The Enigma of William Tell* (c. 1933), a figure with Lenin's face and customary cap exposes his buttocks, with one comically distended). Dalí rejected conformity with the PCF and Soviet communism. He was frank about his fixation on Hitler. An unconventional supporter of Catholicism, Dalí later commended Franco and supported restoration of absolute monarchy, all of which found its way into his art. The story of Dalí is a necessary reminder that explicitly political art can come from all quarters, that reactionary content need not take traditional forms and that radical art can represent paths not taken by history, without being invalid as either artistic endeavour or political proposition.

Situationist *détournement* and Actionism

We can find further substance for future artivism and art collectives in Situationism. In Guy Debord's 1960 "Situationist Manifesto", he opposes "spectacle" (with its echoes of fascistic political splendour) and "preserved art" (as a manifestation of inherited privilege, as defined by J.J. Rousseau). "Against particularized art, it will be a global practice with a bearing, each moment, on all the usable elements. Naturally this would tend to collective production which would be without doubt anonymous (at least to the extent where the works are no longer stocked as commodities, this culture will not be dominated by the need to leave traces)." "[…] Against unilateral art, Situationist culture will be an act of dialogue, an art of interaction." Like all leftists,

Debord sees boundaries as impediments. Once various stages have been enacted, there will be a radical democratisation of art production. "At a higher stage, everyone will become an artist, i.e., inseparably a producer-consumer of total culture creation, which will help the rapid dissolution of the linear criteria of novelty. Everyone will be a Situationist, so to speak, with a multidimensional inflation of tendencies, experiences, or radically different 'schools' — not successively, but simultaneously."[31]

The act of *détournement* (French: re-routing) was one approach advocated by Situationists, which involved the defacing or altering of public signs to undermine the viewers' assumptions. In notable incidents, activists altered posters, once altering "Malboro" to "it's a bore". Later iterations of *détournement* were done by Brandalism, Subvertising, Billboard-Using Graffitists Against Unhealthy Products and other forms of culture jamming, primarily aimed against commercial advertising. This artivism is clearly anti-capitalist in character.

Actionism is an art school that developed in the post-war period, as a response to the tragedy of war and as a critique of the orchestrated grandeur of totalitarians harnessing mass events. The Actionists (with the most notable branch being the Viennese Actionists, which flourished in the 1960s) developed peculiar artificial performances akin to rituals, which involved violence, nudity, sex, pain, blood-letting, mutilation, animal sacrifice, ordure, meat, offal, blood and ordeals of endurance, sometimes including audience participation. It sought to make the audience complicit in spectacles of transgression that were gruelling, shocking, sometimes personally degrading or humiliating. The events — some of which occurred at art venues — were recorded. While these performances lacked a direct social cause, they were intended to give an insight into the savage, primal nature of mankind and to dislocate the spectator from assumptions of morality, nationality and capitalist democracy. It was the most extreme form of a wave of contemporaneous movements of Fluxus, Happenings, performance art, action painting and conceptual art. These movements established the adoption (at least in avant-garde circles) of transgressive performance as a legitimate route for self-expression and social action.[32]

Chicano art, California

Mexican-born Los Angeles painter Carlos Almaraz (1941–1989) formed a collective group of Chicano muralists called Los Four in 1973. Almaraz, Roberto de la Rocha (b. 1937), Frank Romero (b. 1941) and Gilbert Luján (1940–2011) worked on murals relating to Latino history and relating to immigrant Hispanic culture. They made murals to support the contemporary United Farm Workers movement, led by César Chávez and Dolores Huerta. The unionisation and collective movement for workers' rights among migrant workers (primarily in south California) became a national issue. The Neighborhood Arts Programs National Organizing Committee (NAPNOC), a San Francisco automobile workers' group founded in 1967, provided another catalyst. It provided open art classes to San Franciscans of all ages and educational backgrounds, running through the 1970s.[33] At that time, Los Four and associated artists made public art that drew attention to Chicano culture and acted as a focus for community solidarity.

Also in 1973, Judithe Hernández (b. 1948) helped to establish Self-Help Graphics & Art. To this day, it provides access to a print-making studio, materials and tuition for the Chicano community in Los Angeles. Hernández—who attended Otis Art Institute, LA, alongside Almaraz—became the fifth member of Los Four. Hernández explained:

> I think all of us always had a very different vision about what it could be and what it should be, and that's why we fought. Carlos [Almaraz] saw us as a social experiment—in my opinion. He wanted us—I mean, he even had a collective house where William Bejarano and some other people—Leo Limon, I think for a time. They all lived together. They tried to live together in a house in a commune—you know, where you buy food and pay rent and just live like a family in a house. And I think Carlos saw Los Four as well—or he wanted Los

Four and our activities—to be the social experiment to prove that Marxist ideas really were valid. [...] The murals that we did together were collective. Those that we worked together as—I don't think we ever designed one totally on our own.[34]

She added that "now at fifty I feel like I am a painter, I'm an artist, that's what I do, but I didn't feel that way at the time. I was a political being. So were the artists that we knew. We happened to serve the cause through art. We weren't organizers. We weren't other things that the movement needed. We provided them with imagery, with a visual symbol for the issues. That was our job. That's how we saw ourselves."[35]

Las Mujeres Muralistas (active 1974–6) was a collective of female mural painters in California, working on themes similar to those of Los Four and Judy Baca (b. 1946), another notable Chicano muralist. All of these painters took inspiration from Mexican Muralists. Richard Duardo (1952–2014) was a prominent printmaker who worked at Self-Help Graphics and became known as the Warhol of Los Angeles. In the late 1970s, Duardo and Almaraz founded Centro de Arte Público, which was an explicitly political collective, prominently featuring women artists. The Chicano art movement and the women's art movement developed in parallel over the 1970s, sometimes overlapping. Charles Bojórquez (b. 1949), graffiti artist, Linda Vallejo (b. 1951), painter-ceramicist, Yreina Cervántez (b. 1952), muralist, Sonia Romero (b. 1980), printmaker-muralist, daughter of Frank Romero, are all later-generation Chicano artists whose output is rooted in political and ethnic consciousness and who have been notably active in their community, mainly in Los Angeles. Recent artivists have taken inspiration from the Chicano movement's class consciousness and action on migrant and labourer rights.

Art workers united

Artists allying not for collective production but solely for political action is apparent in the associations of the American Artists' Congress (established New York, 1936), NAPNOC (later the

Alliance for Cultural Democracy) (San Francisco, 1967), the Art Workers' Coalition (New York, 1969), the Alliance for Cultural Democracy (Washington DC, 1977) and the Union for Democratic Communication (Philadelphia, 1981). It is worth briefly looking at these.

The American Artists' Congress intended to fight social causes such as "racial inequality, poverty, government censorship, unemployment, global armament, and unfair working conditions for artists".[36] The congress stated: "The Call is to those artists, who, conscious of the need for action, realize the necessity of collective discussion and planning, with the objective of the preservation and development of our cultural heritage."[37] There was a high-minded alliance with the dispossessed and an overt linking of the interests of artists to the plight of the suffering, bracketing artist with manual workers and black people. The organisation called for the extension of the WPA artist-employment programme, which would have materially benefited the participants in the congress. The body's many links to communism led to infighting. When anti-fascism became a national war aim in 1942 and the WPA was disbanded, the body ceased to have a distinct purpose and was dissolved.

The Alliance for Cultural Democracy describes its mission as follows: "We believe in cultural pluralism, and understand the necessity to integrate the struggles for cultural, political, and economic democracy in the United States. The most important initiatives for cultural democracy take place on a grass roots level in communities, neighborhoods, and among activist artists and other progressive cultural workers."[38] The Alliance was originally NAPNOC. NAPNOC relocated from California to Washington DC in the 1970s and worked closely with the Federal Government. The 1973 Federal law the Comprehensive Employment and Training Act (CETA) was established to provide employment skills to the long-term unemployed by sponsoring placement of trainees at local workplaces for between one and two years. In a conscious emulation of the WPA, the San Francisco Arts Commission and NAPNOC used funds from this government programme to provide artists with government-paid jobs in art production. It was (in effect) a WPA-style artist-employment system, created from funds intended to give opportunities to the unemployed. CETA spending on the arts reached $200m per annum in later years. By the time CETA was repealed by President Reagan in 1981, that figure had risen to $300m.

The Art Workers' Coalition—and the associated Women in Art Revolution and the Guerilla Art Action Group (both established in New York, 1969)—was an association of artists, writers and museum staff dedicated to social action, mainly relating to conditions in the art world, particularly in light of opposition to the Vietnam War. Its list of 13 demands to the Museum of Modern Art (issued in February 1969) included: "2. Admission to all museums should be free at all times and they should be open evenings to accommodate working people. 3. All museums should decentralize to the extent that their activities and services enter Black, Puerto Rican and all other communities. They should support events with which these communities can identify and that they control. They should convert existing structures all over the city into relatively cheap, flexible branch-museums or cultural centers that could not carry the stigma of catering only to the wealthier sections of society."[39] In this period, there were a number of protests outside and inside museums.

The Union for Democratic Communications describes itself as "an organization of communication researchers, journalists, media producers, policy analysts, academics and activists dedicated to critical study of the communications establishment, production and distribution of democratically controlled and produced media, fostering alternative, oppositional, independent and experimental production, and development of democratic communications systems locally, regionally and internationally."[40] Its steering committee is comprised of academics but it hosts events that include art topics. It is firmly progressive in its outlook.

Feminism

The goal of feminism is to change the character of art.
— Lucy Lippard[41]

There was no doubt that feminism (in its role as political-advocacy movement) would turn art into a battleground. The Suffragettes had set out that there were no parameters to action necessary in order to bring about women's equality, including violence, suicidal action and terrorism. When the second-wave women's liberation movement commenced in the 1960s, women artists started to see the role of the artist in new ways. No longer wedded to the romantic idea of the lone genius — which seemed to be the preserve of men — new women artists would expound "the myth of solitariness [...] the reality of community".[42] According to the social-constructionist line of feminism — the line closest to Marxism, headed by Christine Delphy — the woman is shaped by social constraints. She is alienated from the fruits of her labour (principally domestic labour) and bound to the source of her oppression: the husband who enacts patriarchal domination, which turns her into property.

Feminists state that all art must be political because there is no division between art and politics. If there were such a demarcation, people would voluntarily relinquish the duty to bear witness to injustice. The authoritarian nature of feminism — like any totalitarian regime or theology — demands that there be no private space, no zone for unscrutinised opinions and no area that cannot be subject to the rigour of feminist reform. "Any discussion of art and politics in art activism today has to begin with the idea that there is no Art which is 'non-political', no art without ideology (even as systems of beliefs and values are challenged or questioned by art, as this is where art's autonomy lies). Chantal Mouffe goes further and argues 'there is an aesthetic dimension in the political and there is a political dimension to art'. Feminism has demonstrated this complex dialectical relation between art and politics many times from the Suffragists to Femen."[43]

"Can we really separate (except perhaps theoretically) art, its imagery and its conscious adoption of thought from Politics in general, from its support systems, when governments continue to fund art institutions and cultural activities as part of their strategy for governance and building civil society, as much in authoritarian regimes as modern democratic ones?"[44] Some feminist art historians decry the concept of the apolitical in art as a sham used to conceal self-interested venality and power control asserted by a male establishment.[45]

Feminism has a long history of advancing its cause through collective action in the arts. Women artists sought to separate themselves from organisations and standards developed by men for men, as they saw it. This meant working through crafts (the minor arts), eschewing the goal of the masterpiece, rejecting the "art-market star system" by acting communally and by taking on politically female subjects (domestic violence, motherhood, sexual expression and so on). Art and political action fused in communal work on installations, exhibitions, cooperatives and publications. This was both solidarity and Marxism in action. The political aim of changing the situation of women led to activism, such as outreach projects on legal rights, domestic refuges, shared childcare, immigrant issues and sexual matters. Filmed street protests extended activism through recordings shown at art events in galleries and social events in shared studios.

Not least, rejection of all hierarchy would embody what was considered a female way of working. Since there had been no female geniuses in art, very well, there would be no need for geniuses at all in future. Communes and collaborations would undermine the commodified nature of fine art by making art anonymously and compositely. Materials would be humble and domestic rather the ennobling ones of marble and oil paint. Quilting with political content would subvert the domesticity of the female sphere. The working process would bond women, reaffirm their agency, fit their cooperative nature and allow them to share rewards. Making art in groups became a common form of feminist artivism in the 1970s and 1980s. There is the conception of leftist political art as deliberately "anti-spectacular", in opposition to aestheticisation of politics (*qua* fascism).[46] This accords with mistrust of beautiful pleasure-giving art found in socialist regimes.[47] Sensuality and delight are refuges from political reality and are therefore suspect to ideologues.

Art related to pacifist causes—again, group projects—entered the realm of protest. Anti-militarism was a feminist staple of the Cold War era.[48] All of this was documented in photographs, films, diaries, memoirs and interviews, to be mined a generation later by academics and writers. Environmentalism informed art-ecological projects of Idle Women, Kinsi Abdulleh, Rirkrit Tiravanija, Agnes Dene, Alana Jelinek and others. From a practical point of view, art collectives or single artists working with volunteers are the most effective way of creating interventions that are large, striking or long lasting. According to the binary (or dialectical) outlook of feminism, women oppose the dominant "male" values: women have an affinity for community (contra individuality), nature (contra science), feeling (contra logic), anonymity (contra fame), generosity (contra greed), selflessness (contra selfishness), anti-capitalism and other values.[49] Art directed by feminist beliefs reaffirms these points, whilst also setting up in opposition contradictory positions of biological essentialism and social constructivism—an irresolvable conflict at the heart of feminism.

Feminist artivist events would be staged as resistance and provocation. Symbolic defiance and absurdity in performances by Sonia Khurana invite ridicule. A sympathetic author describes her performances: "Indian artist Sonia Khurana explores the possibility of occupying space in a body that is raced as South Asian and gendered as female. In the video *Bird* (1999), she stands on a plinth, naked, flapping her arms and legs in a vain attempt to take off. In *Logic of Birds*, she occupies urban spaces in the opposite way to that of the upright, white, colonizing male: abject, vulnerable, grounded, alienated, other, she lies in an anonymous European public space as pigeons peck the ground around her."[50] Action that provokes rejection or indifference is then interpreted as indicative of reactionary resistance or usually as sublimated hostility towards women's speech. So, objections to any specific act of speech (rejecting the message or complaining about its intrusiveness) is presented as evidence of underlying societal bigotry.[51]

Elżbieta Jabłońska makes food as performance art, served to gallery guests in a way that blurs event, vernissage and domestic meal. The Occupy the Kitchen group is "a collective action concerning food sovereignty. *Occupy the kitchen!* is therefore an area of *experimentation and activism*. It wants to be a place where reflection can become action and wishes to examine and expand post-modern consumer *awareness through art and food*. The purpose of this project is to reawaken and energize minds and mouths."[52] On the American Community 2 Community website, one activist "dedicates herself to making sure art and culture are visible and celebrated in immigrant- and farmworker-led movements".[53] Art, artivism, activism, political action and social work form a continuum in this area, with individuals performing multiple roles and paid positions; likewise, certain activities can be interpreted in multiple ways. This is especially true with regard to food artivism, where the practicalities of preparation and consumption for participants are both means and message.

Artivism in action I

We have already encountered some instances of artivism or protoartivism. At this point, we should examine some examples of self-identified artivism in cases where the practitioners explain their thinking.

Anna Matejcek is an artist who has neurological conditions (ADHD and learning disabilities) and sees her practice as a means of communicating her experience and also easing the paths of others who might follow, by informing the audience. "I want my art to spark productive conversations about ways we can reform our educational and societal systems to be more inclusive and open to all people. Ultimately, I would love to see my work widen the way, so that anyone who follows the divergent path after me will encounter less resistance."[54] She described her own thesis as a piece of art. However, illustrations in her thesis of her art—consisting of installations of light sources and crocheted fabric—show her art functions effectively as sculpture/installation/light art/fabric art. Matejcek's art and thesis communicate effectively independently. Whether or not these change viewers' minds is a test all art and texts face.

According to Gail Gallagher, a Canadian touring exhibition (2013–19) highlighting violence against First Nations women had aims including building awareness, promoting change, making connections, ceremonial aspect and unintended benefits. As a First Nations woman, she believed that her own work naturally crossed over between art and action. "Activism through creative art has existed for a long time in the Indigenous community through a number of ways, for example, paintings, sculptures, storytelling and pictures. Through various mediums, attention has been brought to focus on specific issues."[55] This multidisciplinary approach is amenable to adaption to artivism. "Indigenous art activism has played a significant role in raising awareness of the issue of missing and murdered Indigenous women and girl's (MMIWG) in Canada, by uniting various Indigenous and non-Indigenous communities. [… T]he uniting of Indigenous and non-Indigenous communities has created a greater awareness and education of the MMIWG issue, as well as developing an understanding of other serious issues facing Indigenous communities."[56]

The projects "have positively impacted healing for Indigenous individuals, families and communities affected by the issue of MMIWG. The impact of visual art is far reaching, in that they can become a tool that can combat stereotypes."[57] In this case, while the project benefits society in various ways, the project leader does not put a compelling argument that it is best classed as art. The same material and activities could have been toured at solely non-art venues (as opposed to the actual itinerary, which was a mixture of art and community venues) or presented as a social project.

Another project took place in Uganda and was focused on AIDS education. The author of the thesis paper on this was a Canadian doctoral student, who stated the project that she co-led (with a Canadian academic) "engaged with communities to unveil the mechanisms that sustain asymmetrical relations produced by modernity/coloniality in the places We/I [sic] dwell".[58] In her thesis, "co-research is guided by decolonial perspectives".[59] One comparison might be that academics performing artivism in underprivileged districts or developing countries is equivalent to contemporary (secular) missionary work.

One example of street art is particularly effective, as artivism, political messaging and provision of information. At the corner of a building adjacent to a street, a couple of schoolchildren are shown walking together, led by a hand of a figure, around the corner and not initially visible; the figure around the corner is an image of an attractive woman dressed in a skimpy dress and striking an alluring pose. The text above reads "*El 86% de las trabajadoras sexuales somos madres*" (Spanish: 86% of sex workers are mothers). This upsets viewers' assumptions about the nature of the schoolchildren's mother and motivations of prostitutes; it gives factual information. The imagery works very well in its situation, which uses placement, scale and style (monochrome paint applied through stencils) to strikingly convey the makers' points. "Art offers sex worker groups guerrilla tools to achieve political visibility among different audiences. It is also used specifically to fight against the stigma imposed on sex workers, with the understanding that stigma is a collective political problem and not an individual fault."[60]

While some of this work is effective social commentary, there is none—except the last example—where form followed function, turning the means into the message in a way that would have been impossible in any other manner. One can be enlightened and inspired to political action by any art; the label artivism does not change the impact of art-as-art and action-as-action.

Summary

As shown, political art has social functions. Artists have intermittently addressed social concerns with progressive or reactionary intent. Drawing lines between art, activism and political action is not always possible. This ambiguity (and precedents set by art of older eras) allows overt political action cloaked as artivism to enter the area we set aside for the public arts, allowing artivism to assume the status and resources of art.

Case Study

Artivism Against Nazism

Claude Cahun (born Lucy Renée Mathilde Schwob, 1894–1954) and her lifelong partner and artistic collaborator Suzanne Malherbe (1892–1972) worked together on book projects (which Malherbe illustrated using the *nom de plume* Marcel Moore) and made photomontages.[61] Photographs ascribed to Cahun — posthumously recognised as striking examples of photographic performance art — were mainly of Cahun and arranged by her with the camera operated by Malherbe and therefore fully collaborative. The couple (primarily Cahun) were attracted to Surrealism in the inter-war period. As the 1930s progressed, greater political engagement was demanded of alert artists. Impelled by political commitment and artistic proclivity, Cahun became ever more closely involved in the Surrealist movement, specifically the circle around Breton.

In 1932 Cahun and Malherbe joined the Association des Écrivains et Artistes Révolutionnaires, an organisation for communist-supporting writers and artists. AEAR was anti-fascist, pro-communist and non-Surrealist. Relations between the PCF and the Surrealists were complicated and shifting. The Surrealists could not fully reconcile their search for freedom with the PCF and the USSR's increasingly conservative artistic policy. Over the next few years, there opened a division between Trotsky and Breton's position (namely, free creativity by politically alert artists) and the PCF and USSR's directives enjoining adherence to Socialist Realism. Cahun (as she admitted) found it difficult to attach herself to a political organisation, and consequently left in 1933. In 1935 Cahun found herself in conflict with Louis Aragon, who had aligned himself with the PCF and had taken exception to a published statement by Cahun.

In 1935 the group Contre-Attaque was co-founded by Cahun, alongside Breton, Bataille and others. It was an attempt to provide a unified front of Surrealists against fascism. Breton and Bataille had different temperaments. Bataille has been characterised as a proponent of "Left Fascism" — essentially socialism achieved through fascist methods of force, not dissimilar to Strasserism — whereas Breton was a more conventional Marxist. Breton was also an authoritarian who saw Surrealism as his personal fiefdom and he mistrusted the group centred on Bataille's *Documents* journal. Cahun, Malherbe and Breton resigned from Contre-Attaque due to the group's "super fascist tendencies".

In 1937 Cahun and Malherbe moved to Jersey. During the invasion of France in 1940, the British government demilitarised the Channel Islands as indefensible and evacuated much of the population. Cahun and Malherbe remained in the expectation of German occupation, with the intention of performing active resistance. Their house was requisitioned by the German army, yet still they engaged in small acts of subversion that carried a severe penalty. They smuggled food to starving slave labourers building defences and retained a radio after a ban was imposed, passing on war news verbally.

The couple decided to oppose the Germans with subversive activity, something doubly risky for them. They were associated with the anti-fascist Surrealist movement, though they had used pseudonyms; Cahun was half-Jewish. Additionally, they were newcomers to the island, with relatively few friends or potential protectors. Their defiance was at first routine. Malherbe concealed the fact that she spoke German — defying compulsory-notification orders. They refused to hand in their camera, radio or an inherited pistol. As the German restrictions on Jews increased, Cahun's secret identity became more of a burden. Yet it was Cahun, stubborn dissident and committed anti-fascist, who persuaded Malherbe to help in a campaign of subversion and defiance.

They tore down posters and swivelled signposts. They left messages in German on scraps of paper and cigarette papers; they wrote them on walls. They made subversive photomontages. They combined tactical clarity with wit and creativity, using different colour tissue paper for different kinds of typewritten messages. A sample message read: "Down with Hitler! Down with the non-German vampire who guzzles the blood of our young people! Down with war!"[62] They played on the consciences of the soldiers rather than insulting them. "Lucy and Suzanne did not address the residents of Jersey, nor did they even write in English. Instead, they spoke directly to the German soldiers themselves, appealing to them in their native language as good German men. They hoped to divide the soldiers from their leaders so that the rank and file would desert or even mutiny."[63] It was not so distant from pre-war Surrealist games aimed at disconcerting the bourgeois, but this time the consequences were potentially lethal. Many islanders were gaoled for defiance, some were deported to forced labour camps. Jews and half-Jews faced deportation to concentration or death camps.

The couple became more daring by slipping notes into tunics, boots or briefcases of German soldiers. They smuggled food and news to foreign prisoners building sea defences on the beach near their home. Soldiers and their horses were billeted at their house for some months, forcing the couple to act with extreme caution. They took in a fugitive Ukrainian who had escaped from the labour camp. In July 1944, the Secret Field Police raided their home. Finding incriminating notes, Cahun's diary and the typewriter, they arrested the women. Cahun was tortured. The couple were imprisoned apart and each took an overdose of phenobarbital. Both survived and Malherbe would attempt suicide a second time.

They were kept in solitary confinement for months, during which time Malherbe built a rapport with a kindly guard, who shared information and would do favours. She could speak to him in German and he became a vital link to the outside world even though there was a degree of suspicion between them. Prisoners passed information on scraps of paper pushed through ventilation tubes and holes in walls. Their deportation to the continent was forestalled by the Allied victory in Saint-Malo. The German occupiers were now cut off from mainland Europe.

In November 1944 the women were tried. They were tried for listening to the radio, having a weapon and camera and distributing anti-German propaganda. The trial revealed that the Germans had been worried by the subversive activities, thinking it denoted widespread discontent in the ranks of the soldiers. Found guilty, they were sentenced to death. It seems that the Germans did want to carry out the execution and that there was no expectation that so late in the war two (relatively) elderly women would be executed. The pair were convicted and sentenced to death, something they had fatalistically expected. They refused to plead for clemency. Even their gaolers were dismayed at the sentence and officials on Jersey made efforts to reduce the penalty. Then orders came from Berlin: sentences to be reduced to 10 years servitude. It was something of an academic point, as Germany was rapidly approaching capitulation. The women even heard from soldiers that their propaganda had struck chords with them. On 8 May 1945 all surviving prisoners were freed.

Much of the couple's personal archive and collection of art, books and letters had been burned by the Gestapo, obscuring their activities. Disillusioned by the perceived passivity of islanders regarding the occupation, the couple lived on in Jersey, with Cahun's health failing. She died in 1954. Malherbe died in 1972.

The proto-artivism of Cahun and Malherbe was genuinely transformative and radical; it required bravery but allowed room for creative subtlety and humour; it had a firm ethical position. The actions destabilised in a way that was of value to the artists and the wider community. It never impinged on anyone else's access to resources nor curbed the free speech of others. It was one of the few ways in which resistance could be advanced in a way that was both artistically and politically meaningful, done in the face of the greatest danger.

Two

State Art & Utilitarianism

This chapter will outline how and why public cultural institutions were founded, how the state taking responsibility for funding altered the dynamics of organisations and how the rise of utilitarianism in government programmes opened the door to cultural entryism. The public museum and art venues have always been targets of anti-traditionalists. The fall of museums is both complicated and simple. Various factors combined to allow planned subversion of arts bodies but also fortuitous chance played a part. From their conception, public museums contained inherent contradictions that left them open to takeover.

Museum principles

Rationalist and materialist principles established by Francis Bacon, René Descartes, John Locke and David Hume came to form the Enlightenment. The Enlightenment gave rise to acceptance of scientific method, which (when considered in relation to the study of mankind) encouraged the collection of data. Disinterested appreciation and neutral recording of information about artefacts was part of the empiricism of a secular mapping of humanity and history as part of a project to comprehend all. Jeremy Bentham's pursuit of "the greatest good for the greatest number" posited expanded access be applied not only to the collection of artefacts and information but to their accessibility to the population through libraries and museums. Monastic, university and private libraries—and the private museum, in the form of the *Wunderkammer* or royal/ancestral collection[64]—had existed for centuries before but the acceptance of universalist principles by prominent gentry, enlightened clergy and academics led to the foundation of public forms of picture galleries, libraries and museums. Sir Hans Sloane's bequest to the nation of his natural history collection and library in 1753 became the foundation of the British Museum, British Library and the Natural History Museum. The Alte Pinakothek (established Munich, 1779), Uffizi Gallery (Florence, c. 1789), Louvre Museum (Paris, 1793), Dulwich Picture Gallery (London, 1814) and the National Gallery (London, 1824) brought art that had been the preserve of the wealthy and powerful to any member of the public able to pay a penny. Soon, every self-respecting nation had a national collection of history, nature and art, held in trust in perpetuity for the people.

Thus, as the modern nation state encroached on the functions of the monarchy, aristocracy and Church, so *noblesse oblige* was replaced by the duty of an enlightened bourgeoisie, industrialists and landed gentry to donate to, fund and organise artistic, historical and scientific collections held by the state on behalf of people, open to the public. With these museums came some of the nascent values of national patrimony in an era of state-owned culture. No longer would collections be personal accumulations of items acquired by individual men, but instead rational and thorough assemblies; contents would be selected to illustrate a grand narrative of the subject. Collections had to be of a high standard, treated with care, not misrepresented and comprehensive (or at least representative) within the bounds of the collection's remit and the nation's resources. They should also be public, within reason. (There are exceptions, such as various state archives of diplomatic or security papers and forbidden-materials collections in libraries; in these cases, access is restricted due to concerns regarding legality, ethics and morality.) Associated principles were observed to varying degrees by institutions, sometimes driven by the character of the nation's elites. For example, allowing artefacts to leave public collections by way of deaccessioning is treated variously as necessary, welcome, permissible and forbidden, regulated by precise laws. American attitudes towards deaccessioning are somewhat flexible; British institutions are largely regulated by national laws which (largely) forbid deaccessioning.

Regrettably, there is not space in this book to adequately discuss the matter of deaccessioning as a tool of artivists and decolonialists. Suffice to say, removal of materials is a key tactic of radicals, whether that is removal of nudes from art galleries, statues from public squares or books from school curricula. Artivism, iconoclasm, deaccessioning and decolonisation are all interlinked and overlapping fields for action by cultural entryists. The focus of this book is the positive addition of new cultural material/action rather than negative retraction of old cultural heritage, but it is worth bearing in mind that progressive artivism of today is complementary to campaigns to restrict, censor and destroy manifestations of older culture. Artivism is often explicitly positioned as an assault on the status quo, demanding retraction or dismantling of customs, institutions and material. Artivism is one modern-day manifestation of iconoclasm.

It is common for publicly-funded organisations to operate with an arm's-length principle. Management and policies of organisations regarding operations, personnel, projects and expert decisions are supposed to be shielded from the influence of politicians. That is intended to protect organisations from outside influence, political bias and corruption, so that they serve the public in a neutral manner. As we have already seen in the case of the ICA, once organisations are under the control of cultural entryists, application of pre-existing rules, standards and expectations to the bodies is recast by entryists as meddlesome politicians violating of the arm's-length principle in order to suppress free speech and using bodies to promote regressive values. If regulators are amenable to blurring boundaries between government and museum (and between art and politics), then rules are not enforced. That is the prerogative of the elite and we call it corruption.

Public arts: evolution or subversion?

The origins of Arts Council of England (ACE) were in the Council for Encouragement of Music and the Arts in 1940, an effort to improve morale and sustain the cultural life of Great Britain during extraordinary circumstances. In 1946 this was reconstituted as a permanent body of the Arts Council of Great Britain (broken into regional boards in 1994). Its 1994 Royal Charter sets out ACE's objects: "(1) develop and improve the knowledge, understanding and practice of the arts; (2) increase accessibility of the arts to the public in England; and (3) advance the education of the public and to further any other charitable purpose which relates to the establishment, maintenance and operation of museums and libraries (which are either public or from which the public may benefit) and to the protection of cultural property; and (4) advise and co-operate, where it is appropriate to do so, with the Departments of Our Government [...]"[65] It has powers "to make grants and loans for charitable purposes [and] establish funds".[66] The ethos of ACE is not set out in the Charter but it is clear from the body's statements that the arts to be supported would be those in need of support—the non-commercial, avant-garde, artistically important, nationally significant and historically valuable. ACE always sought to balance the self-serving nature of its elitist concerns with fulfilment of non-controversial service.

In the USA, the National Endowment for the Arts (NEA) is "a public agency dedicated to supporting excellence in the arts, both new and established; bringing the arts to all Americans; and providing leadership in arts education".[67] It was established in 1965 as part of the Great Society social programmes, a subsidisation of worthy causes. Made possible by a landslide electoral mandate, these programmes were intended to link Democrat-instituted beneficence with projects for urban, deprived and non-white constituencies.[68] While ACE originated from a wartime coalition government and a post-war agreement that the arts in a devastated economy required encouragement, the NEA was explicitly a project of the political left, imposed without bipartisan agreement. Although ostensibly neutral, as a concession to liberal allies in the arts[69] and an appeal to an urban electorate neglected by arts provision, the NEA was progressivist in outlook, as previous arts programmes had been.[70] Artivists have admitted that the NEA's public-arts funding was (depending on one's viewpoint) subverted or diverted: "[...] artists and administrators, in collaboration with NEA program staff, were able to make use of the (deliberately) vague principles contained in the Endowment's founding documents to fashion a fundamentally new, and in many ways progressive, model of arts funding policy."[71] American artists in the 1980s and 1990s saw the contraction of NEA funding as a direct assault by Republican lawmakers on progressive art.[72] This was not an inaccurate view, as conservatives acknowledged.[73] American left-wing artivism in this period was reaction (or mobilisation) against a threat to their livelihoods and access to public venues.

The rise of utilitarian thinking in government regarding the arts was to some degree already seeded in the patrician ideals of government-funded arts programmes. Once a programme is established, the argument for its existence has already been won, which changes priorities. Expansion of an entitlement is mission creep. Consider: an arts programme must be established to help bring high-quality arts to the people; this arts programme supports artists, let's get these artists to help promote healthy living to their audience; this arts programme promotes good health, how can we make this join up with existing government initiatives? And so forth. The arts programme becomes part of an integrated state apparatus for social control in a planned economy. This happens not intentionally but due to bureaucratic imperatives.

As with perennial questions about staying true to a country's foundational documents and principles (the two not necessarily synonymous), the issue of programme evolution or subversion is an endless debate. Does not the provision of a one-time bailout or tax set a precedent that ensures it will not be a one-time-only event? This is why, when the National Lottery was founded by the British Government in 1994, profit was reserved for ACE, heritage and a few charities. It was ringfenced specifically to reserve income for "additionality", i.e. the funds could not be used to replace money that would have been spent by government, it must be used to do extra work. It could not be diverted into other areas, such as health, education, housing and so forth. This remains largely the case, although somewhat diluted.

The principle of additionality is to specifically separate the fund from general departmental spending. To the argument "How can you spend money buying a Van Gogh painting when a children's hospital needs new scanners?", the response is not primarily moral but legal: the law states this money cannot be made available for medical equipment. This prevents the government from raiding the fund to compensate for errors in its usual budgeting or from pandering due to panic or patronage. The obstacle is not an ethical argument but a legal device to forestall erosion of both principle and practice of art funding remaining reserved for the arts.

State-led art and utilitarianism

As venues become more enmeshed in the demands of ACE and local government, so they become more detached from independent artistic assessment and more prone to managerialism. Many art-venue directors have backgrounds in the leisure sector and local-government bureaucracy rather than art production or criticism. This fosters tendencies in managers to defer to consensus, avoid giving offence and seek benign solutions. Pre-emptive censorship is not unknown.[74] With annual grant renewal on the minds of administrators, adventurous programming is almost impossible. The administrative class does not always need to impose quotas or encourage artivist programming because the unspoken consensus of the public-arts monoculture is the state's most effective tool of control.

The creeping expansion of the state leads to a tipping point: the state as main arbiter of taste. Rather than retrospectively collecting the best art of every period, the state attempts to direct art of the day. The values of all states are self-serving. A Western state wishes to maintain parliamentary democracy (without consensus-breaking parties), ethnic/cultural/sexual plurality, placidity, stability, compliance, orderly consumption, progressivism, globalism, erosion of tradition, environmental anxiety and atomisation of society; above all, the state wants to avoid any overt threat from powerful ideologies impervious to moderation, such as nationalism, nativism and religious fundamentalism. Art that Western states promote accords with these aims. Artivism is ideal. It is commissioned, made and consumed by members of a left-liberal administrative class that controls the state.[75] It is generally a temporary spectacle, so it leaves only a trace and is mediated by texts and photographs. On a large scale, it requires the permission of legal authorities. It asserts the rights, wealth and generosity of the state. Dissent against the elite's values does not enter public-art venues, at least in any other than the most ambiguous or mild forms, because it would never occur to public commissioners to accept such material. There has never been a piece of publicly-sponsored artivism that encouraged viewers to be less anxious about the environment, advocated fidelity within marriage or celebrated traditional marriage. Perhaps that would make for dull art but there has been plenty of dull artivism promoting the opposites; maybe we should offer conservative artists a chance to counter-programme.

Once a state becomes the leader in art production, avenues for utilitarianism proliferate. Utilitarianism is a consequentialist system of ethics, which holds that rather than absolute ethical positions or laws being instituted and applied, consideration must be given to the outcome of any law. The guiding principle becomes, what is best for the greatest number of people? It is relativist and pragmatic. As an ethical system, it is flawed due to its flexibility, permitting a subject to justify any action as more beneficial than not. It has been criticised as "a recipe for preferring expedience to justice".[76]

Since benefits of cultural activity accrue incidentally, why not measure and direct them? For decades, the economic advantages of centres of culture have been studied; today, art venues are integral to regeneration plans. Under influence and direction of central government, local councils, NGOs and charities, art venues can be deployed to functionalist ends: as hubs for education, multiculturalism, mental health, social improvement, community cohesion, social integration, immigrant outreach, environmental awareness, tourism, even centres of vaccination. Inevitably, such calculations alter the mission of an arts venue. A quandary is how much attention and budget should be devoted to the core tasks of acquiring, displaying, conserving and exhibiting art compared to new social tasks, which have evolved from considerations to priorities.

To meet the guidance of ACE and to secure an adequate budgetary allowance, managers must have in mind percentages and audience figures. The percentages and figures of certain activities and demographic minorities must be as high as possible and always rising. Artivism becomes critically important because it seemingly (by current standards) meets the primary role of art presentation, plus one or more secondary roles. For example, an artivist project celebrating refugees falls under art provision, celebrating multiculturalism, social integration and immigrant outreach. It therefore allows administrators to meet many commitments through one action and one expenditure. This gives artivism an inherent advantage over any display of apolitical painting or sculpture. Likewise, in an era when such matters are monitored and rewarded, compared to a majority-demographic creator, the minority-demographic creator is always preferable for administrators.

It is simplistic to characterise the common institutional bias against majority-demographic creators (white, non-migrant, heterosexual, male) as aversion or hatred when it is not solely (or not even) those. It is in part motivated by administrative calculations of a system set up to paternalistically assist the allegedly disadvantaged; it is a system that generates its own incentives to discriminate against majority-demographic creators at every opportunity. With no mechanism to counter this discrimination—and no recognition that such discrimination may be unjust and counter-productive—the pattern persists. For the most unapologetic progressives (those who espouse Critical Race Theory), racism is prejudice plus power and thus it is impossible to be racist towards a majority. Therefore, there can be no discrimination because majority-demographic individuals cannot be victims of racism.

In recent years, reports from art insiders have extolled the extra-cultural benefits of art museums. A report produced for the Museums Association and ACE in 2013 examined additional roles for museums: "Promoting economic growth through tourism, investment and regeneration; facilitating individual development through education, stimulation and building skills; facilitating academic/expert research; promot[ing] happiness and wellbeing; fostering a sense of community; helping the vulnerable;[77] protecting the natural environment." The following are "purposes challenged by the public":[78] "providing a forum for debate; promoting social justice and human rights".[79] Despite knowing of the resistance of the public, staff are reluctant to relinquish activism.

Here are some additional roles.

Art for urban regeneration: A member of staff at the Tate assessed the urban impact of the establishment of Tate Modern. "From the very start of the Tate Modern Project, we sensed and hoped that we could breathe new life into an important historical area of central London. To make this work, we set about building relationships to widen our impact beyond the building itself." He compared this to the work of

> [...] colleagues in Medellin, Colombia who have used escalators and public libraries to give poor mountainside communities both physical access to their homes and places of cultural congregation along the way. I think of Nantes, France, where arts and culture are central to their city and economic

development plans. Meanwhile, in Rio de Janeiro, Brazil, in the shadow of the Maracena stadium, Contemporary Dancers are sharing facilities with carnival performers, thinking, talking and educating each other in an inner-city community. And in Rotterdam, Netherlands, the City Museum is working with the city and its communities as its "muse". These are all local projects, but they are also important far beyond their immediate localities.[80]

Art for community outreach: An education officer at an American museum wrote about how his experiences of museums had led him to become an artist initially.

> If it hadn't been for a museum's commitment to community outreach, and its desire to create worthwhile programming for teens, I can say that I have literally no idea where I would be today. When you're a teenager, who you are is still in flux, and as a result the future can seem terrifying. Coming to terms with your identity as an artist and your place within the art world is daunting, even for adults. We know the grim statistics about arts funding, especially in the underfunded public school systems of our nation's larger cities. More and more, it falls on us as cultural institutions to pick up this slack and create safe, creative environments for this next generation of artists to flourish.[81]

Not least, the creation of the position of education officers has led to a common perception (within museums) that such staff do not have to limit their work to explaining art but can also perform the functions of mentors and social workers.

Art for social cohesion: A lecturer at Vanderbilt University has expressed her conviction that museums perform a unique role in multicultural districts.

> Museums have the capacity to enhance social cohesion, which is the product of a trusting, connected community. History museums and historic sites, in particular, can serve communities by stimulating dialogue on difficult issues, accurately

representing all the people of a nation, and creating forums for discussion among groups with disparate opinions. History museums promote social cohesion by solidifying the identities of their audiences—as members of communities, ethnic groups, nations, and the world.[82]

Although her emphasis is upon the history museum, similar ideas have been advanced regarding fine art, with one 2021 report stating, "the arts are indispensable for their power to build community with unique depth and meaning".[83]

Art for immigrant integration: One project in Ontario state in Canada used writing a graphic novel to educate about (and counter) domestic violence against women within the Muslim migrant population.[84] An Italian academic paper recommended that integration of immigrants should be the responsibility of local cultural authorities. It was "of paramount importance to implement those integration policies, involving both immigrants and residents, that maximise the potential positive contribution of immigrants to economy and society. Museums and cultural institutions have historically played an instrumental role for stimulating socialization and intercultural dialogue. Cultural policy is recognized as a powerful tool for promoting immigrants' integration in the present."[85]

Art for economic growth: In the USA, museums were estimated to have brought in $50bn during 2019.[86]

> [...] The museum sector is also essential to the national economy—generating GDP, stimulating jobs, and contributing taxes. These economic effects can be measured using a standard technique known as economic impact analysis. This kind of analysis measures not just the direct (operational) contribution of the museum sector but also the impact that is felt as its activities ripple out across the economy.[87]

Art for tourism:

> For many years museums were ignored by the tourism industry. However, the trend is reversing and today,

museums are attracting a large number of people. They are one of the favourite choices in the world of travel and leisure. A growing number of museums is the major driving factor for the growth of museum tourism. From classical art museums to museums that tell the story of great pride of a particular nation, the number of museums worldwide are increasing. Museum is a part of education and education does not only depend on books but also on the presentation of information. Several paintings and sculptures in museums provide useful information and insights to visitors as they are representational of the culture and heritage of a particular place and its people. An interest by foreign tourists to explore the culture of a particular place through museums is fuelling the growth of the global museum tourism sector.[88]

Art for mental health: As Angus Kennedy put it: "The Towner [Museum, Eastbourne] at least seems unclear whether it is a museum of art, medical clinic, remedial unit or nursery."[89] Over recent decades the issue of mental health has come to fore. Beyond recognising the serious problems of mental illness, professionals in healthcare, psychiatry, therapy, education and social services sought to apply their ideas to wider society. The Western state (yearly entrusted with ever more of the well-being of citizens, employing a civil service willing to micro-manage individual lives) and the cultural sector (dependent upon state patronage and seeking more public money) expanded into the mental-health field through art-for-well-being. By 2018, an expert judged that, "Wellbeing represents a key element of policy-making in the UK government's Department for Culture Media and Sport and this has stimulated a growing body of evidence on the relationship between the visual arts and wellbeing."[90]

A report to examine the benefits of art for participants' mental health concluded: "[…] engagement in the visual arts for adults with mental health conditions can reduce reported levels of depression and anxiety; increase self-respect, self-worth and self-esteem; encourage and stimulate re-engagement with the wider, everyday social world; and support in participants a potential renegotiation of identity through practice-based forms of making or doing."[91] Unsurprisingly, the author of that report recommended greater consideration, research and resources for his specialism. "National and local policymakers should ensure that the partnerships of mental health professionals, artists and researchers are more adequately resourced, properly sustained, and informed by consistent and recognised evaluation methodologies and frameworks."[92]

The recent loan of a Monet by the Courtauld Institute to Ferens Art Gallery was marketed as a mental-health event remediating the impact of Covid-19 lockdown. The press release read:

> "The practice of mindfulness and the importance of mental health really came to the fore during the lockdowns, so I'm delighted to see that this exhibition and its accompanying events programme has been designed to encourage conversation about these issues, especially amongst young people", says Councillor Brabazon, Hull City Council.[93]

The National Gallery sent a flower painting by Jan Van Huysum to "the walled garden mental health and wellbeing hub in Perth".[94] In 2019, the National Gallery sent its recently purchased self-portrait of Artemisia Gentileschi on a tour of a women's library, GP's clinic, secondary school, prison and a second library. The tour seemed part social outreach, part restorative justice, with a feminist subtext. Artemisia's personal fortitude is given as reason enough to admire her, regardless of her actual achievements.[95]

Making and viewing art does have positive effects upon people. It is also undeniable that specialists, artists, venues and states have self-rewarding reasons to pursue provision of arts for mental health. It is difficult to disentangle motives and weigh benefits to an audience compared to costs and drawbacks for providers. Further lies the question of how much we lose in terms of agency and resilience by expecting the state to provide anodynes and tranquilisers in a society made stressful by pressures partially imposed by that state and its agents. After all, the best way to obviate the distress of lockdown is not to provide art but to lift (or never impose) lockdowns.

Abandoning detachment

At least one artivism supporter (Korpe, 2013) quotes George Orwell as justification for politicisation of art bodies. Korpe wrote: "George Orwell once wrote, 'All art is propaganda'. In his essay The Frontiers of Art and Propaganda (1941), Orwell stated that: *it is impossible to divorce a person's creative output from their political biases and ideological outlook, and that 'our aesthetic judgments are always colored by our prejudices and beliefs'.*"[96] However, when one looks at the full essay, Orwell is making quite a different point.

> [The mixture of politics and literature in the 1930s] destroyed the illusion of pure aestheticism. It reminded us that propaganda in some form or other lurks in every book, that every work of art has a meaning and a purpose — a political, social and religious purpose — that our aesthetic judgements are always coloured by our prejudices and beliefs. It debunked art for art's sake. But is also led for the time being into a blind alley, because it caused countless young writers to try to tie their minds to a political discipline which, if they had stuck to it, would have made mental honesty impossible. The only system of thought open to them at that time was official Marxism, which demanded a nationalistic loyalty towards Russia and forced the writer who called himself a Marxist to be mixed up in the dishonesties of power politics.[97]

In other words, authors abandoned supposedly apolitical attachment to pure literature in order to criticise fascism, but this required giving up independence by aligning with Soviet Marxism. "Just as many writers about 1930 had discovered that you cannot really be detached from contemporary events, so many writers about 1939 were discovering that you cannot really sacrifice your intellectual integrity for the sake of a political creed — or at least you cannot do so and remain a writer."[98] Orwell says here that abandoning the aspiration of objectivity meant authors sacrificed their integrity, not least because the Soviets (whom they supported) formed an alliance with Nazi Germany in 1939, which made clear that realpolitik manoeuvring betrays supporters.

Korpe states that since detachment is impossible for artists, politics should be embraced in art. Orwell states that politics compromises the artist both as an artist and a person *qua* political agent, writing elsewhere in this essay that to assess literature apolitically is a difficult but admirable aspiration. Postmodernism views language as a mediator of power, controlling thought and society, reinforcing hierarchies. As seen in this case, postmodernists seek to justify their disparagement of objectivity (and attempts towards impartiality) partly in order to discredit their opponents and remove obstacles.

Trust in museums

In 2017, an American survey showed that trust in museums was relatively high. Of American respondents, 73.7% trusted art museums, 73.2% history museums and 74.2% science museums, compared to 64.8% trust in NGOs and 59.1% in government agencies.[99] (A British survey of 2020 put trust in museum curators at 82%.)[100] Responding to the American survey, museum consultant Jim Richardson conducted a survey of people's attitudes to museum campaigning. The survey revealed that when asked "Do you believe that museums should have something to say about social issues?", 27.5% of respondents replied "yes" and 31% "no". "However the number of people who felt that museums should have something to say on social issues changed depending on how much a person had interacted with a museum in the past 12 months." Frequent visitors were more in favour of campaigning.[101] The more a person was attuned to current trends in museum policy, the less resistant he/she was to campaigning by museums, suggesting that exposure to institutions influences audience expectations. "Visitors under the age of 30 were more likely to think that museums should speak up about social issues. 38% said they believed museums should do this while 42%

answered 'maybe'." Younger people (more supportive of social activism) saw less of a problem with museums campaigning.

Richardson concluded: "This would further point to a real hunger in the under 30 age group for museums to be more activist."[102] It can be inferred that these young people expect to encounter programming that confirms their views on topics such as "homelessness, inequality and the environment". Discussion of artivism cites putative consumer demand for such material, which aligns with the progressive expectations of consumers, staff, creators and consultants, all largely members of the liberal-left elite.[103]

High trust in museums presents an opportunity to activists. If their propaganda can enter museums, thereby reaching a new audience and receiving the imprimatur of trustworthiness, their cause will be advanced. This makes museums a prime target for activists. Entry also acts as symbolic capture of a stronghold of the putative opponent of the activist.

Richardson writes, "Museums are seen as trusted institutions and that political capital is especially important if museums wish to influence social change"[104] (this is confirmed by a survey that shows museums are seen as less politically biased than other organisations[105]). Although Richardson sees this trust in museums as capital to be expended on political issues, he does not consider that museums have this trust in the first place because they are seen as impartial and apolitical. If such capital were to be spent, then the esteem for museums would decrease, the way trust in the mass media has plummeted as the more overt the media's political bias and censorship has become. Once that capital is spent, it is gone. One only has to look to the widespread distrust regarding the mainstream media to see the future of museums should they embrace politics.

Crisis of the public-funding model

The co-option of resources (funds, venues, prizes, grants, salaries, exhibitions) earmarked for purely (or primarily) cultural or aesthetic activity by political activists presents a major crisis for the public-funding model. The arm's-length principle is that political figures and organisations should not exert direct influence or patronage over cultural activities carried out by independent bodies that are financially supported by the state. That principle assures the public and arts bodies a degree of security and stability; it assures above all that politicians will not have undue influence over the arts.

This has been the consensus position in the UK since 1945, when various national programmes supporting the arts were founded. Or it was until the 1990s and the creeping acceptance of the utilitarian principle. That principle states that cultural production has practical benefits beyond enjoyment and general education, including the aforementioned social cohesion, immigrant integration, community outreach, urban regeneration, economic growth, tourism, mental health and other factors. These are measurable and controllable and should be considered in the foundation, direction, programming, promotion and funding of arts bodies. It says that it is correct—indeed, necessary—for interested parties to influence or control arts bodies with these considerations in mind.

According to philosopher Benedetto Croce, "Art is not concerned with the True (as logic is) nor the Useful (as economics is) nor with the Good (as morality is). It has its own object, the Beautiful, that stands independently on equal terms with the other three. [...] True poetry must have no utilitarian, moral, or philosophical agenda."[106] This is the art-for-art's-sake argument. This position was taken up by the Decadent Movement and the Aesthetic Movement, both of which were in their heydays in the late 1880s and the 1890s. Until recently, this connoisseurial consideration was paramount in selection and presentation in art.

The difficulty is that once the utilitarian principle is accepted, it allows political influence to be imposed externally (by politicians, NGOs, donating charities and pressure groups) and internally (by activist staff) in order to allocate resources according to non-artistic criteria. If arts bodies are now to be made utile, then it simply falls to the most able, wily or dominant parties to get a slice of the communal pie. It becomes a free for all, as advocates of causes seek to capture and protect resources. No longer is politics implicit in the content of art, it is explicit in the provision and allocation of public resources for the arts. This means that criteria which should be primary to producers and administrators of arts —competence in execution, merit in content, aesthetic worth, intellectual coherence, seriousness in purpose, artistic integrity, beauty, originality—become secondary or tertiary to practical, financial and sectarian concerns.

Worse still, once instrumentalist aims are admitted, targets-culture administration demands that arts venues become ever more effective tools for social change, which means venues become less neutral. With art-for-change a priority, art-for-art's-sake is not a viable position, thus tipping the balance towards utilitarianism. Viewing art for pleasure becomes too much of an indulgence, too much a shirking of responsibility to confront the social realities of exclusion, poverty and racism. If we do not refute the legitimacy of utilitarianism as a governing principle, we perforce reach a version of Socialist Realism, when apolitical art was denounced as "bourgeois formalism" and removed from the walls of museums, to be replaced by paintings of grain harvests and revolutionary heroes ratifying the constitution. Art that is enjoyed for its beauty cannot compete with documentation of suffering refugees or displays of health advice. Why should not a museum become a hub of education or economic activity? How can we object to a museum acting as a vaccination centre, place of worship or food-distribution point? Even now, if one takes artivism as legitimate, soup kitchens, raves and legal-advice drop-in centres can be art. Artivism is a way in which unskilled artists in search of resources exploit utilitarianism in arts bureaucracy, framing it as high-status avant-garde art and claiming political kudos by adopting the elite's preferred causes. In crude terms, it is unemployed artists pretending to be social workers for the satisfaction of bourgeois art administrators and consumers.

In the postmodern age, we are taught that nothing is apolitical. There is no such thing as impartiality and that advocating neutrality as an ideal is simply protecting the oppressive status quo through disingenuous calls to consensus. It is better to expose the political workings of society and address them plainly. We are all political beings, so arts bodies must be political. Politics must be acknowledged in the content of art and its selection. Why shouldn't curators seek to use their power to give a platform for the unvoiced and marginalised? Following that logic, we can see biases of curators in the causes they consider worthy. Yet how is the "social awareness" of curators any different from the "power patronage" progressives and postmodernists decry? Curatorial support is simply paternalistic privileging of preferred parties, no different from that of the Athenian state, Medici princes, nineteenth-century industrialists and authoritarian regimes. In a qualitative sense, it does not matter that progressive curators support black urban collectives and that millionaire bankers bankroll solitary abstract painters; both arbiters distribute capital to institute patronage on the bases of political preference, influencing the market and demonstrating social status. Rather than exposing and taming political patronage, postmodern strategies accelerate it.

A deeper issue arises when curators allocate public money on the provision of social goods judged by allegiance to their politics. This has implications beyond a private individual allocating his own money. "Everything is political" but not every political view is equal nor even valid, it seems. Today's curators—ostensibly given positions due to their competences at managing funds to provide art as a community service—have set themselves up as arbiters of politics, as well as of culture. In the West, it is clear that only political viewpoints from the centre or the left are considered eligible for public funding. As discussed previously, public venues in the UK never platform events/displays that advocate the primacy of Christianity in contemporary Britain, question (much less actually oppose) mass migration, reject multiculturalism, support reinstatement of the death penalty, portray abortion as morally wrong, question the narrative of imminent environmental crisis, agitate for imposition of a worldwide

Islamic caliphate, among other issues. Whether or not one finds these views incorrect or repugnant—they may be, I take no stance on them here—it is undeniable that a significant part of the population holds one or more of these views. Yet the elite forthrightly rejects such views without hesitation.

Some voices are more authentic than others; some groups are more worthy than others; all art is political but not all political positions are legitimate.[107] The art establishment will arbitrate what is acceptable. Political art, community activity, non-art events and artivism can and should exist—outside publicly-funded art venues. There is limited space and resources for public art and thus there is utility in restricting activity in art venues to display and discussion of art works that roughly conform to the traditional fields of fine art. If a commercial gallery, private museum, corporation, cooperative space or community centre wishes to devote resources to artivism, there seems little reason to object.

Politics in art will always exist. It is best articulated in an honest and serious manner. When it is presented in a publicly-funded art venue, that should preferably be at time when it has become historical. Artivism—no matter how worthy the cause nor how personally sympathetic one may be towards its intentions—never has a place in a publicly-funded art venue.

Summary

The public museum was always vulnerable to institutional capture. It was flawed by relying on continuous transmission of the canon and aesthetics in order to allow the public to appreciate fine art and the importance of art museums. This practice was essentially erased by the relativism of postmodernism, timidity regarding praise for Western civilisation and institutional capture of schools and universities by progressives. The core of the public museum rested on accepting the principles of Bentham, primarily that museums do good by serving the public. By the end of the twentieth century, the state effectively controlled arts bodies; it was in a position to determine what "serving" meant and policymakers determined that serving the public was best measured by utilitarian standards. Institutions founded to preserve and transmit essential values were turned into devices to erase those values.

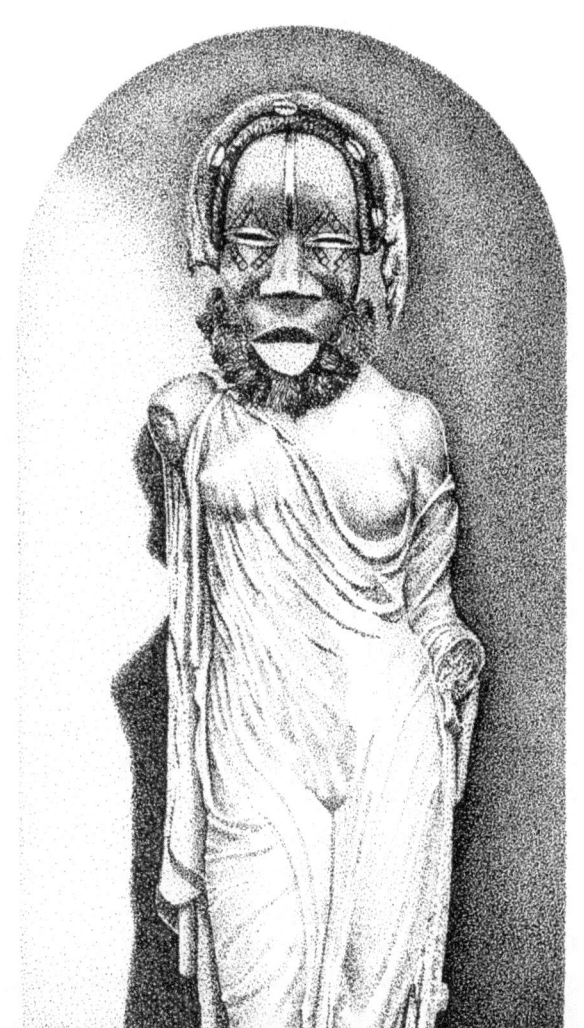

Case Study

Banksy, Cosy Artivist

In the 1990s, a series of cut-outs of rats appeared at street level on London buildings. The rats wore chain necklaces and baseball caps; they had portable stereo boom-boxes; they posed as thieves, spies and subversive agents. These anthropomorphised rats were criminals and rebels, standing in for graffitists, ravers and drug dealers, the overlooked. They represented the resistance, in all its anarchistic, working-class grubbiness. The detailed, precise stencil designs displayed wit, frequently using the physical location for impact and irony; they poke fun at authority in the form of the police and big business such as banks. For their creator, the subhuman underclass was transposed into rats in his art. "If you are dirty, insignificant, and unloved then rats are the ultimate role model", said Banksy.[108]

Banksy established his signature style around 1994. He used photo-derived stencils and black and white paints to make pithy motifs of everyday life. He says he adopted the stencil approach (not an original one) in order to cut down the painting time and reduce the chance of being caught.[109] An alternative version came in a 2002 interview, where he admitted he simply was not good enough to cut it as a freehand graffiti street artist.[110] As his stencil style has become well known, he has used his signature less often. His style has become his signature. Banksy would never have become a national figure without a presence in London, where he moved in 1999, shortly after painting his largest piece in his native Bristol—*The Mild Mild West*, which shows a teddy bear throwing a Molotov cocktail at riot police.

Another Banksy trope is irreverent children with paints. For him, children are embodiments of the free spirit of humanity and act as truth-speakers. His children represent hope by undermining authority, disrupting adults' consumerist assumptions and dissolving walls—specifically the security wall separating Israel from the Palestinian Territories (discussed below). Some pieces are outright jokes, with fake trapdoors painted on the walkways of bridges and walls designated "authorized graffiti area". Later, more elaborate, pranks included a fake ATM spewing £10 notes with Princess Diana's image and a telephone box mangled and impaled by a pickaxe (this latter sold at a charity auction for $605,000).[111]

Many of these interventions were temporary and expected to last only a few days until council workmen come to paint over the walls. Most exist only in photographs. In recent years, it is just as likely that a property owner (including local councils) will have the wall surface preserved behind plexiglass or cut away and taken to the nearest art auctioneer or gallery dealing in street art. Artivist pranks included pictures surreptitiously positioned on museum walls by Banksy or a collaborator. These interventions lasted only a few hours, until the interventions were spotted and removed. Again, these interventions are recorded in photographs which have been widely published, not least in books dedicated to Banksy's art. The museum plants were planned like bank robberies in reverse, with the artist thinking how to position an item and get out unapprehended. The stunts earned widespread news coverage.

Banksy's everyman art was taken up with alacrity by a popular press baffled and bored by the art of the Turner Prize. Banksy's art is accessible, understandable and reproduces well in print. Add to that the aura of a Scarlet Pimpernel of the counter-culture and the press have readymade copy for slow news days. When Banksy sprayed cows and pigs with graffiti in non-toxic paint, he made sure to tip off animal-right campaigners. Their predictable protests generated the required publicity.

Banksy broke into mainstream recognition in the USA when his 2006 Los Angeles gallery exhibition (which included a live painted elephant) reputedly made £3 million in sales; among the collectors were Angelina Jolie and Brad Pitt. Shepherded by agent Steve Lazarides, Banksy's star rose and with it there was a rebirth of street art as a commercial presence, following the early 1980s first wave of street art in galleries. The artist has donated generously to charities connected to welfare and poverty and has also supported dissident artists. He has given valuable works to charity auctions. Yet Banksy is far from an anti-capitalist rebel. He sold prints from his early years at whatever prices he could get, unaware that art prints are not produced like posters but are printed in strictly limited editions. One suite of Banksy prints was sold as limited to 250 copies but actually many more were produced and sold, misleading buyers.[112] Later editions have been printed in such an ambiguous fashion. To describe this as "disorganised editioning" is perhaps the most generous description.[113] His studio churns out replica variants on an industrial scale.[114]

Studying Banksy's work in depth, certain social attitudes become apparent. Policemen are thuggish goons or inept clowns serving repressive governments. Graffitists are individualists battling conformity. Old people are bitter conservatives and closet bigots. Children are enlightened seers of truth. Consumerism is deadening; capitalism is exploitation; authority is control. The real defacers of public space are advertisers.[115] Classic fine art is stuffy and out of touch. With such adolescent attitudes, Banksy's satire could hardly be anything other than stale. Painting attack helicopters over an English pastoral scene and portraying a Monet pond filled with dumped shopping trolleys is schoolboy stuff. (Established fine artist Peter Kennard's version of Constable's *Haywain* with Cruise missiles was just as feeble when it was discussed as social critique in the 1980s.)

To understand Banksy, one has to go back to his native Bristol of the 1980s and early 1990s. Banksy formed his political outlook in a city that is a hotbed of left-wing attitudes, from community activism and student politics to rave culture and non-conforming lifestyles. It was an obvious place for graffiti to develop into elaborate grand-scale street art. Being an anti-authoritarian progressive is utterly conventional in Bristol. When protestors stand in Bristol's College Green with signs welcoming migrants, they face not riot police, skinhead gangs or conservative ridicule but sympathetic students and thumbs-up from bus passengers. Banksy was born in 1973.[116] His identity was revealed in a newspaper article in 2008 but since then the press has since largely respected his wish to remain pseudonymous. The only detail from Banksy's life that is relevant here is that he went to a public school and is far from the working boy made good that he is portrayed as. A friend says, "He went to one of the poshest schools in Bristol."[117] Banksy himself has never explicitly said in his interviews (conducted by phone or email) that he is working class, so it would not be reasonable to accuse him of deception.

In the early 1990s Banksy became involved in a group of graffiti artists working in Barton Hill, Bristol.[118] Playing down his middle-class suburban origins, he found an emotional home in the cannabis-smoking, risk-taking, anti-authoritarian milieu of working-class Barton Hill graffitists ("graffers")[119] working in the Bristolian anti-government-action and rave/trip-hop scenes. His early freehand efforts were competent but unremarkable. His art did not stand out until he adopted the stencil technique. His early efforts are not reproduced in official Banksy books. Part of Banksy's folk hero status comes from his anonymity (or pseudonymity). The moniker "Banksy" developed from his first alias "Robin Banx". The use of a street name is a way of claiming authorship without revealing the true identity of the author — someone who commits acts of criminal damage. "Banksy" proved to be both a catchy street name and brand name.

As Banksy's profile has risen, attitudes to his art have changed. This type of graffiti is now a cool addition to the neighbourhood and a landmark for hipsters and tourists. It adds a touch of class to the gritty urban chic, complementing the ethnic grocery shops and gang violence. Today, despite having few commercial galleries, "Bristol has more working artists than any other city outside London."[120] The majority are street artists not fine artists. Bristol is now marketed as a tourist destination with guided tours of the street art, featuring the few remaining early Banksy paintings.

Museums find high-profile artivism a draw in terms of publicity and attendance. In 2009 an exhibition of 100 pieces and interventions by Banksy was held at Bristol City Museum and Art Gallery, financed by the artist and arranged in great secrecy. It proved a great hit, attracting over 300,000 visitors and was the second most popular exhibition in the UK that year. Thus, artivist and art establishment mutually benefit from platforming artivism in a museum setting. A film about Banksy's art was released in 2010. *Exit Through the Gift Shop* is an examination of the street-art scene and also about Banksy. It showed him cutting stencils, painting and talking about his work.[121] That same year *Time* magazine chose Banksy as one of its list 100 most influential people in the world.[122]

On 21 August 2015, Banksy's theme park Dismaland opened in Weston-super-Mare. Dismaland was planned as a cruddy, inept, cut-price British version of the cheery American theme parks. It was an art-project-cum-entertainment featuring recognisable Banksy motifs, art by well-known artists made specifically for the display, humorous installations, deliberately "crap" merchandise and various jokes. The staff were deliberately off-hand, bored and uninvolved—which worked because both staff and visitors were aware of the in-joke. Banksy wisely decided to limit its run (which closed 36 days after it opened), which contributed to Dismaland being sold out throughout its operation. It was very popular and by all accounts thoroughly enjoyed by the majority of its 150,000 visitors. Dismaland worked because it was a pop-culture circus. This is what Banksy is good at—amusing, diverting and providing flippant commentary on everyday life in entertaining events. Whilst that falls short of art, it is not an insignificant skill.

Yet however rebellious Banksy is depicted, his outlook is locked in unexamined assumptions of his teenage years. Consider Banksy's work on the wall around the Palestinian Territories. One interpretation of the West Bank Wall is that it is an aggressive imposition upon the Arab population of Israel, which deprives them of free movement and humiliates them ("The most politically unjust structure in the world today", according to the artist).[123] Another interpretation is that it was a necessary security measure that has curbed the wave of terrorist suicide bombings and knifings of Israelis. Banksy's trope of children who represent innocents seeking freedom appears in one image of a girl carried over the wall by a bunch of balloons. Fair enough, but what about Israeli girls who had to live in fear of rocket attacks on their schools and are now provided with more security by the wall? Banksy's humanitarianism does not seem equally distributed between Israelis and Palestinians. In this, Banksy is in lock-step with British progressive partisan support for Palestinians. It seems that the street artist saw photographs of a pristine wall and thought of how to poke fun at authority; he never got around to learning the complexities of the situation.

From an artistic point of view, Banksy's stunts—including breaking into zoos and stencilling enclosures—could seem needy and vain, but we should remember that Banksy is at heart a graffer; only in ambition, scale and notoriety is he different from those vandalising high-rise towers and railway embankments. However, Banksy's natural tendency towards conformity draws him to the coffee-table book and the West End gallery, occasionally reasserting his street cred with a new wall stencil. The glibness of his ideas is a limitation for an artist but a positive necessity for a street artist who deals in pithy memorability. Banksy lacks most of the characteristics of a serious artist: originality, complexity, universality, ambiguity, depth and insight into human nature and the world generally. Banksy is a talented graphic designer with a flair for self-promotion, one who makes one-liners that are mildly amusing, sometimes clever, but never more than one-liners. Banksy's art lends itself to newspaper reproduction or style-journal pages and was done (in early years) to capture the eye of editors of those publications. His iconoclasm is jokey temporary publicity stunts. None of Banksy's interventions create lasting damage or significant cost to remove – most portable interventions are removed and sold immediately – and he has never caused authorities more than mild inconvenience.

The essential problem is not that Banksy holds unexamined prejudices or that he is mediocre as an artist; it is that he is lazy. He never truly challenges us because we can predict his positions on all topics. It is symbolic of a lack of public critical thinking that Banksy has grown so famous without his art being repeatedly exposed as not only shallow and conventional but also derivative and occasionally plagiarised.[124] Banksy could never have become as famous and rich as he is without his audience – comprising fans, book-buyers, periodical editors, collectors, gallerists and museum administrators – sharing his political outlook. Despite cultivating the air of a rebellious outsider, Banksy is a cosy artivist and a tool of establishment politics who reflects back to the liberal-left middle class their every assumption.

Three

The Managerial Elite & Artivism

This chapter sets out several attempts to analyse the nature of the elites and how their technocratic-utilitarian outlook on the public arts leads them to support artivism as a means of applying their values, directly and indirectly.

James Burnham's managerial elite

In the books *The Managerial Revolution* (1941), *The Machiavellians* (1943) and *The Suicide of the West* (1964), American political theorist James Burnham (1905-1987) advanced a critique of Western-style democratic capitalism. His conclusions were striking and pessimistic. Although rulers and the elite pay lip service to democracy and party politics,[125] the elite remain in power as an oligarchy. The managers—different from capitalist entrepreneurs and small-business owners—accrete power by curbing free markets and traditional centres of alternative power. The circulation of the elites (allowing the ascent of exceptional individuals) permits the persistence of equilibrium; when this is impeded, disequilibrium leads to violent adjustment, including rival elites gaining power. Circulation causes ideological creep in the same way that cycling of generations educated according to new distinct beliefs also does. This is not necessarily related to the Long March Through the Institutions—which saw incremental institutional capture by leftists—but could incorporate such a process. Minorities have an advantage over majorities in terms of cohesion, in-group preference and organised action.[126]

Political scientist Gaetano Mosca outlined the principles:

> In reality the dominion of an organized minority, obeying a single impulse, over the unorganized majority is inevitable [... T]he minority is organized for the very reason that it is a minority. A hundred men acting uniformly in concert, with a common understanding, will triumph over a thousand men who are not in accord and therefore be dealt with one by one. Meanwhile it will be easier for the former to act in concert and have a mutual understanding simply because they are a hundred and not a thousand. It follows that the larger the political community, the smaller will the proportion of the governing minority to the governed majority be, and the more difficult will it be for the majority to organize for reaction against the minority.[127]

George Orwell summarises *The Managerial Revolution*:

> Capitalism is disappearing, but Socialism is not replacing it. What is now arising is a new kind of planned, centralized society which will be neither capitalist nor, in any accepted sense of the word, democratic. The rulers of this new society will be the people who effectively control the means of production: that is, business executives, technicians, bureaucrats and soldiers, lumped together by Burnham under the name "managers". These people will eliminate the old capitalist class, crush the working class, and so organize society that all power and economic privilege remain in their hands. Private property rights will be abolished, but common ownership will not be established.[128]

Fascism and communism were two alternative routes to the same end: convergence of all power (political and economic) in the hands of managers. What would replace free-market capitalism would be an amalgamation of government and industry. "The truth is that, whatever its legal merits, the concept of 'the separation of ownership and control' has no sociological or historical meaning. Ownership *means* control; if there is no control, then there is no ownership."[129] The expansion of the state's legal powers necessarily prevents owners from being able to exert full control over property, instruments of production and money. "When, finally, the major part of the instruments of production come under governmental ownership and control, the transition is, in its fundamentals, completed. The 'limited state' of capitalism is replaced by the 'unlimited' managerial state. *Managerial society* has taken its place."[130]

Orwell criticised Burnham's books when they were published during World War II.[131] Orwell's case partly rested on Burnham's inaccurate prediction of a German victory, based on Nazi Germany's more efficient managerial organisation. Orwell contended that, whatever advances managerialism was making in Europe and the USSR, it had left the USA a haven of free-market capitalism. Yet, with the New Deal and (after Orwell's death) President Johnson's welfare state, increasing corporate regulation, expanded federal oversight of banking and subsidisation of firms (even whole industries)[132] at federal and state levels, Burnham's analysis has become measurable reality. In return for legal protections,[133] immunity from prosecution,[134] partner status[135] and subsidies,[136] large corporations have become integrated into the work of the US federal government to an extent that making distinctions between public and private ownership is sometimes impossible.[137]

In *The Machiavellians*, Burnham mined elite theory (derived from Machiavelli, Mosca, Sorel, Michels and Pareto) to outline the nature of his managerial elite as an extension of governing elites those writers had previously analysed. He concludes, "The primary object of every élite, or ruling class, is to maintain its own power and privilege. [...] The rule of the élite is based upon force and fraud. [...] The rule of an élite will coincide now more, now less with the interests of the non-élite."[138] In *The Suicide of the West*, Burnham warned that Western civilisation was receding due primarily to internal weakness, which he ascribed to liberalism (outside of the American terminology, this is better called progressivism or leftism).[139]

What is important about Burnham's analysis for us is that it explains why the state (via its client class of art administrators and artists) fuses politically advantageous art with action against the values of the working class. Note that the managerial elite is not dependent on capitalism; in fact, a vigorous capitalist economy decentralises power, asserts primacy of the autonomous rights of individuals (and companies) to own and trade property and resists authoritarian top-down control, hence the managerial elite seeks to constrict the free market. The managerial elite is not tied to any economic system; it thrived successfully in mixed economies, fascist regimes and communist states.

Alternative elite theory

Eva Etzioni-Halevy presents an alternative liberal analysis of the relationship between elites,[140] sub-elites and the public in Western democracies. This is democratic elite theory, developed in the shadow of Marxist class analysis that gained precedence in sociology and politics in the post-war period.[141] "What class theory has disregarded is that it is neither classes nor organizations, but rather elites and sub-elites, who conduct the actions usually attributed to classes or organizations. Both so-called class actions and so-called organizational actions are, in effect, elite actions."[142] This is not the elite theory usually discussed. "[... D]emocratic elite theory is not in the confines of *the* elite theory proper in the tradition of Pareto, Michels or Mills. Rather it follows the liberal tradition of thought, introduced into the social sciences by, for instance, Max Weber, Joseph Schumpeter and Raymond Aron. But it is still *an* elite theory."[143]

Etzioni-Halevy stresses the competition between different elites: "[...] elites have always shown a tendency to subjugate other elites, the relative autonomy of elites has never been assured [...]"[144] Unlike Burnham's elites, the democratic elites are constrained by separation of powers in democratic societies at the same time as they constrain the range of options available through control of major political parties. "[... D]emocratic principles defend an elite and sub-elite."[145] She notes the way the system of democracy is of value. "Established elites generally have a common interest in the maintenance of the system from which their elite positions derive."[146] The elite does not necessarily mean only those in official positions of power in institutions. "It means that, by this definition, elites are not only some of the most advantaged, but also the *most active men and women among the disadvantaged*, or those who champion the interests of the disadvantaged. Elites therefore include those who are the most active in preserving the inegalitarian, elitist structures, that is, the status quo, but also those who are anti-elitist and struggle for change towards greater equality."[147]

Etzioni-Halevy discusses the co-option of protest, which we might apply to artivism. "I suggest [...] that the strategies devised by Western governments for the purpose of coping with the new social protest movements in the last few decades have been most prominently those that employ positive rather than negative sanctions. [...] And among the positive devices the most prominent has been that of co-optation, of incorporating elites of social movements into existing power structures in exchange for moderation."[148]

We do not need to assign moral values to various groups or theories discussed above, though readers will have their own sympathies and responses to elite theory. The subsequent text explains how elite theory sheds light on how certain ideas and practices in art have gained widespread acceptance in the face of common scepticism and hostility from the public.

Anatomy of the managerial elite

Who comprises the managerial-elite class in the arts? One definition could be that it is literally "those who manage". To be more specific, we can identify some demographic traits and sociopolitical views common to this group.

1) *Female*: Women are demographically over-represented in the cultural sector generally and arts administration specifically. A report of 2014 had 63.3% of major museum staff and 55.2% visual arts staff as female.[149] The reporting of 2018 found that women comprise 56% of the workforce in the overall arts sector in the UK.[150] The Arts Council of England has a National Council comprising of 53% women and its overall workforce was 65.7% women.[151] In the UK, 53% of directors of museums and non-commercial venues are women.[152] The ratio is even stronger in the USA.[153] In the UK, more women than men participate in the arts[154] and visit museums.[155] More woman-led organisations received visual-arts grants in the UK, compared to male-led ones.[156] Due to various factors, women are more predisposed than men towards treating art in instrumentalist ways and using art as a tool for social change.
2) *Anti-Brexit*: While 52% of voters supported Brexit, in the creative industries 96% opposed it.[157] The left was opposed to Brexit more than the right.[158] Before the 2016 EU referendum, 479 MPs opposed Brexit, 158 MPs supported it.[159] The cultural sector was strongly opposed to Brexit, with leading figures recommending against voting Leave.[160] Ninety percent of British fashion designers opposed Brexit.[161] Of the British technology industry, 87% opposed Brexit.[162] Major international organisations almost unanimously warned against Brexit.[163] This is mirrored by the editorial selections of the BBC, the UK's largest broadcaster and commissioner of cultural material. Contributors to BBC news and current events programmes were overall opposed to Brexit.[164] Fifty-four percent of UK academics do not want to associate casually with Brexit supporters; 37% admitted they would discriminate against job applicants because the applicant supported Brexit.[165]
3) *Left wing*: In a study of American academia, faculty staff self-described as liberal (left) outnumber conservatives 12:1.[166] At one top Ivy League university, 99.5% of all political donations went to the Democrat Party.[167] British academics

overwhelmingly voted left (Labour/Liberal Democrat/Green parties: 75%; right-wing parties: 20%).[168] Left-wing sympathy tends to correlate with opposition to Brexit, though there is a strong old-left, anti-capitalist argument in support of Brexit.
4) *White*: In the UK, the public arts are consumed by a greater percentage of the white population than of the minority-ethnic population, comparatively.[169] Of individuals employed in the art-music-performance sector, 5% are non-white,[170] compared to 12.8% of the overall UK population (as per 2011 census).
5) *Middle or upper class*: The upper/middle class engage with arts significantly more than the lower class. In the UK, 85.3% of upper socio-economic group engaged with the arts per annum, 67.3% of the lower socio-economic group; property owners: 81.8%, private tenants: 80.9%, social/council tenants: 60%.[171] This is even more marked in art museum and gallery attendance: upper socio-economic group: 61.6%, lower: 39.5%; property owners: 57.4%; private tenants, 53%; social/council tenants: 31.5%. When museum staffing is reduced, volunteers became a larger proportion of the workforce. These volunteers and interns are usually middle class.
6) *Less patriotic, more republican*: The elite tends to be unrepresentatively left leaning and opposed to nationalism and monarchy.[172] Of Labour supporters, 48% were ashamed of British history. Only 29% of Labour supporters were proud of British history, compared to 53% of the general population.[173] Most Labour supporters would like to see the monarchy abolished (53%), whereas the general population is 63% pro-monarchy.

There are other aspects which may pertain but for which we have little or no statistical data. The establishment elite (and by extension, the public-arts sector) is predominantly atheist, anti-Christian, pro-multiculturalism and supportive of state intervention, economic controls, free-speech restrictions, censorship and subsidies.[174] These attitudes — along with expected views on migration, abortion, capital punishment, etc. — tend to be associated with the typology established above.

This data shows that the top politicians, broadcasters, academics, culture-sector leaders and business executives share a distinct outlook, one that is different from that of the general British population.[175] Arts administrators (and artists who collaborate with them) share common aims and social values with the elite; their interests naturally converge. As an economist observed, subsidies in art (ostensibly for all) tend to accrue to the main consumers, the middle class. "[... T]he average taxpayer pays for the consumption of upper-middle class art consumers and therefore income is redistributed in an unwelcome direction."[176] Subsidies serve the distributing elite, rather than the citizens from whom the payment is extracted. Whether the arts administrators understand this is uncertain and is largely veiled to them: "[... I]t's questionable whether artists and art lovers deliberately and strategically try to put pressure on the government in order to receive the benefits of art subsidies."[177] Administrators signal their high status by programming material embodying elite taste. Administrators, artists and consumers in the subsidised arts come from the same class and share many attitudes; their interests are aligned; intentionally or otherwise, they reject tastes and values of non-consuming groups, even though these groups partly fund the public arts.

There is no evidence to suggest that the tendencies listed above—atypical at a population level—will be countered in future. Indeed, considering social science on how monocultures develop, the expectation should be that this trend will continue until all conservative or reactionary perspectives in the public arts become either excluded or silenced. Support for artivism (on grounds of utilitarianism and the "diversity, inclusivity, equity" agenda) within the commissioning class is rooted not only in mission statements of arts organisations, staff status-signalling and hitting budget-sensitive quotas but in the outlook of staff. Unless countered, artivism will expand throughout the cultural sector.

Artivism in action II

American performance artist Allan Kaprow defined the genre of Action Art (not to be confused with Actionism or Action Painting). According to Kaprow (who also coined the art term "Happening"), Action Art was "nonart" that was "whatever has not yet been accepted as art but has caught an artist's attention with that possibility in mind... Nonart's advocates, according to this description, are those who consistently, or at one time or other, have chosen to operate outside the pale of art establishments—that is, in their heads, or in the daily or natural domain."[178] *FOOD* (1971–74) was a project founded by Gordon Matta-Clark. He established an artist-led cooperative restaurant in SoHo, New York City, called FOOD. A different cook would run the restaurant every night and FOOD functioned as part business, part performance, part artist discussion centre. One participant remembered:

> The artists who were attracted to SoHo came from all around the country, and the world, working in all areas of the arts. They didn't mind living primitively on the fringes of society in exchange for roomy studio space. There were many different political theories and social theories, ethnicities and aesthetics —but everybody was opposed to the [Vietnam] war... and the establishment... We felt that all institutions were aligned with "the establishment," and so they needed to be turned upside down and reevaluated.[179]

A well-known example of artivist social work is Tim Rollins + K.O.S. (Kids of Survival). Tim Rollins (1955–2017) trained as an artist and was employed as a school teacher in the Bronx, New York. It was there, in 1982, that he began to lead collaborations between at-risk teenagers who called themselves K.O.S., who produced large art works and groups of pictures with a political or social slant. The art was exhibited widely and led to income for the artists. Some of the K.O.S. went on to have solo careers.

Artivism can provide effective metaphors. SpY's *Crisis* (2015) consisted of the word "CRISIS" spelled out in €2,000 worth of 2-

cent coins affixed to a wall in Bilbao. It was picked off the walls by beggars, vagrants and immigrants within a day. That spectacle worked as a pithy embodiment of the plight of the poor. It may lack subtlety and intellectual coherence but, as a visual statement and a conceptualisation, the event worked well.[180] "[SpY's] aim is always true, without ever losing sight of that magical simplicity of his. His work is a complex catalogue of heart-wrenching truths", according to one writer.[181]

Artivists can tell the stories of the overlooked. Here is an extract of an interview with Doris Salcedo (b. 1958):

> My works are for the victims for violence. I try to be a witness of the Witness. I look for an intimate proximity with the victims of violence that allows me to stand in for them. One must feel close to another in order to stand in for him or her and create an artwork out of another's experience. [...] To accompany someone to his or her death, step by step, opens us to the other, and leads us to forget our own existence, it unites us to that other, who will then remain inscribed inside us. The exhaustive investigation that I carry out on the deaths of the victims of violence, on the actual deed of the murder, leads me to accompany them, step by step, to that death, and in that sense I feel as though they are inscribed in me.[182]

Some artists (including Jorge Rodríguez-Gerada)[183] subvert posters in the spirit of Situationist *détournement*, or they imitate posters (Jenny Holzer, Barbara Kruger). Such artists work internationally, as do lesser-known ones. "[Sharon] Hayes continued the performances across Europe, including in Brussels, Warsaw, Vienna, and Paris, carrying signs translated into the native language. She documented the performances with 35mm slides and later showed the entire series of performances at the [New York] Guggenheim [...]"[184] Backed by dealer Jeffrey Deitch and crowdfunder Heliotrope Foundation, Swoon's interventions have been hosted in New York, San Francisco, Berlin, Lisbon, Venice, Haiti, Israel, Brazil, Melbourne, Mexico, Kenya, Tunisia, Tokyo and other locations. Artivism provides artists with subsidised travel and the aura of being a world-famous cultural figure.

Delaure and Fink define one branch of artivism, called "culture jamming". According to them, culture jamming appropriates existing mass culture and subverts it; it is playful and often references high culture; it is often anonymous; it is participatory; and it extends itself through replicability and serial forms that can be applied by anyone to other subjects/targets. It "implies an interruption, a sabotage, hoax, prank, banditry, or blockage of what are seen as the monolithic power structures governing cultural life".[185] This is more towards the anti-capitalist and anarchist end of the spectrum, dealing with pop culture and business. The Yes Men successfully spread the hoax that Dow Chemical (parent company of Union Carbide) would fully compensate victims of the Bhopal chemical accident, forcing the Dow Chemical press department to admit they would not be paying compensation.[186] Such stunts sometimes cross the line into assault, such as Biotic Baking Brigade's throwing pies at public figures.[187] However, comic and non-dangerous these actions were, they still consisted of physical attacks, ones that were treated as justified by those who disapproved of the subjects — a precedent for 2016's "Punch a Nazi" meme and attacks on political candidates in the USA and UK.[188]

Artivism as a tool for rival power elites

The managerial elite has a consensus of values. Discussion is limited to specific policies, speed of implementation and preferences regarding party and personnel to act as the front of a largely uniform body.[189] The elite seeks to implement its vision, suppress opposing ideas and discredit any competing elite. In the West, the main acceptable targets (as designated by the elite) are nationalists, populist nativists, reactionaries and religious fundamentalists. Libertarians and socialists are not opponents but unwitting allies who can be used to weaken traditions and institutions that present resistance towards the managerial elite's advancement of homogenisation, globalism, technocracy, atomisation and planned economies impervious to democratic dissent.

As we have seen, the most prominent artivism is broadly in line with the sensibilities of the managerial elite in the West. Artivism is used by the establishment, but it is value neutral and is a tool, receptacle or vehicle for any political message. It is untrue to state artivism is a route to greater justice; it could just as easily be used to spread prejudice, hatred, fear and lies, just as propaganda can be. Art is as amenable to deception as it is to revelation.

It is worth giving an example of progressive artivism which comes satirically close to endorsing the reactionary. *Sokkomb* (2009) by collective IOCOSE was a self-assembly guillotine. It was designed to look like an IKEA product and placed surreptitiously in IKEA stores. It was intended to satirise calls for capital punishment in response to mass illegal immigration and violent crimes committed by illegal migrants in Italy. However, the creators did not get the plaudits from art-literate liberals that they had expected. "The point of *Sokkomb* was to test to what extent IKEA consumers would be shocked by the prospect of a cheap tool for DIY justice. Eventually, only a few people reacted with surprise or disgust, while many seemed to be seriously interested in buying the product."[190] In some cases, we find ostensibly progressive creators flirting with reactionary positions under the cover of satire, benefitting from praise and patronage from both progressives and reactionaries. In this case, it was privileged progressive creators mocking the impotence and fear of a population facing crime and social strife and thereby (inadvertently) revealing a deep divide between population and governing elites.

This raises a tantalising question. Could a reactionary rival power elite use artivism as the current elite does, but against that incumbent power group, potentially using the ambiguity between satire and endorsement? We already know about the division in values and style found in the sensuous *Ancien Régime* rococo and austere republican neo-classicism in the 1780s leading up to the French Revolution. The question is, could artivism be used the way painting was then? One can infer that should a subversive power elite seek to undermine values of a ruling group, it could use artivism as easily as other methods, including propaganda, misinformation, entryism, education, erosion, language framing and subversion. Indeed, traditionalists and reactionaries consider that is exactly how the current progressive elite gained ascendency. It is ironic—but completely expected—that it was liberals who opened museum doors to leftism by granting artivism legitimacy. Once leftists dominated politics and organisations, liberals saw their values of tolerance and plurality assaulted with alacrity.

Would right-wing artivism be feasible? The conservative and reactionary would use artivism purely instrumentally because they would not consider actions to be art. Setting aside artistic claims for artivism, artivism-as-action and artivism-as-consciousness-raising are both viable models for anti-progressive causes. Subverting governmental advertising through alteration, vandalism or memes is already a widespread, grassroots, spontaneous response. So much so that the European Union issued a report denouncing memes as weapons ideally suited to irreverent reactionaries.[191] It concluded: "The violent fantasies that are woven into these witty narratives may function as serious accelerants of mass violence that need to be countered as such."[192] The "It's okay to be white" meme is one that was especially effective because progressive negativity towards it exposed double standards—a supposedly egalitarian movement celebrating black racial consciousness but condemning white racial consciousness. Humour works very effectively at angering elites and undermining their narratives. Memes reveal a power dynamic—with peripheral but numerous conservatives on the outside making fun of a progressive elite in control of state resources and mass media—demonstrating that progressives dominate institutions but cannot command the respect and obedience they demand of the population. Potential reactionary appetite and competence in the field of artivism remain undetermined because no reactionary has been afforded significant funding or platforms.

Video-sharing, crypto-currency and peer-to-peer decentralised networks—plus crowdfunding—could all be used to grow counter-establishment artivist networks. After all, P2P Foundation is a diffused online network, designed to allow peer-to-peer communication, leftist in outlook. Its twin aims are to agitate for de-growth (economic contraction) and subverting copyright restrictions ("commons").[193] Its platform hosts calls to accelerate eco-activism and dismantling capitalist democracies through artivism. Such systems could be used against progressivism.

Summary

Many apparently subversive artivist actions are expressions of elite values (against the views of the majority population), which are backed by the establishment, which shares those values. The elite advances domination of culture through artivism, using artivism as a vanguard movement to undermine tradition and majority values. There seems no reason why dissident artivism of a nationalist, nativist, conservative and anti-progressive character should not successfully undermine the incumbent elite's narrative.

Case Study

Extinction Rebellion, Handmaiden of Technocracy

Thomas Sowell has written[194] of a recurrent pattern among the intellectual and political elite: crisis (identification of a problem in need of remedy), solution (top-down, usually tax-funded policies or new regulatory agency), results (results fail to meet expectations, problem persists), response (supporters explain that funds or policy were insufficient). To these we can add three following corollaries: lack of responsibility (supporters are not held to account), new issue (supporters move to a new issue, partly to alleviate a problem related to the previous one), cycle repeats. No issue in the West has been more pressing for the general public in the last 40 years than an apparent worldwide environmental crisis caused by mankind. Measurements of global warming, melting polar ice coverage, rising sea levels, atmospheric levels of carbon dioxide, deforestation, extinction of wild species and depletion of fish stocks have been taken as proof that imminent and irrecoverable environmental catastrophe poses an existential threat to mankind.

Extinction Rebellion (commonly abbreviated to XR) is an eco-activist movement dedicated to direct action in order to force radical social, political and economic changes in order to avert environmental collapse. XR was co-founded in April or May 2018 by Roger Hallam, Gail Bradbrook and others, to act as a spearhead for eco-activist groups Rising Up! (of which Hallam and Bradbrook were members) and Compassionate Revolution Ltd (of which Hallam is a director). The draft manifesto made public by Rising Up! presents anti-capitalist, anti-debt, anti-growth and pro-welfare-state policies.[195] It calls for corporations to be abolished "to be replaced by worker-owned co-operatives that don't seek profit or growth".[196] Both Rising Up! and XR claim there will be a catastrophic collapse in civilisation that will result in survivors reverting to tribal nomadism—a vision (seen through their eyes) as bucolic as it is alarming. The predicted eco-collapse seems to be something these campaigners welcome, even though they publicly work to avert it. Rising Up! is clear in its hostility to the police. "A Rebellion does not ask permission from the police; it understands that the police are a fascist organisation who are enforcing a racist, patriarchal neoliberal system."[197]

XR is different. In the XR handbook (published by Penguin Random House) you will find—sprinkled among personal stories and grave statistics—easy-to-follow guides on to how to undertake activism and protest. XR advocates non-violent mass protest, along the principles established by Gene Sharp.[198] It says change is possible through peaceful disruption and that it is the sight of normal protestors being arrested that will precipitate a wave of public sympathy. Hallam suggests that involvement of "1-3 per cent of the population"[199] is sufficient to topple a government.[200] Although the aims and beliefs of the three groups are interchangeable, XR presents itself as less threatening than the older groups. It is as consciously shaped as a brand. "Unlike many of the spontaneous social-media-fuelled rebellions and uprisings in recent years, Extinction Rebellion has been carefully planned. For several years a group of academics and activists have been working on two main questions: Why have we failed so miserably to stop climate change? And how the hell are we going to stop it? […] We studied decades of work looking at organizational systems, collaborative working styles, momentum-driven organizing and direct-action campaigning."[201]

XR ties itself to issues of social justice. It uses slogans ("System Change Not Climate Change") that are taken from the *Socialist Worker* and Socialist Workers Party.[202] The aim is to rule through Citizens' Assemblies (overseen by experts) with an environmental priority.[203] XR tends to shy away from making explicitly anti-capitalist statements in published material. For example, in the XR handbook (a masterfully crafted piece of propaganda), there are calls for reduction of environmental exploitation by companies but not a single proposition on behalf of anti-capitalism—a core tenet of Rising Up! and Compassionate Revolution. When anti-capitalist sentiments come out in spontaneous social-media posts of XR leaders, they are usually subsequently deleted.[204] XR keeps silent its eco-socialist views because it needs to appeal to the masses. "It has to be fun", urges XR's co-founder.[205]

Artivism is a component of XR campaigning. It has created spectacles that catch the eye and are reproduced in the mainstream media.[206] On 11 August 2019, a group of red-clad figures with white faces appeared at a beach at St Ives, Cornwall, to warn of rising sea levels. It was timed to cause maximum impact among the many tourists. A professional-quality video of the event was produced. Similar costumes appeared in October 2020 for a silent theatrical performance outside the Australian Parliament as it debated an environmental bill. Another performance was at the June 2021 G7 summit in Cornwall. A different approach is provision of interactive festivities such as a "late-night playground", allowing visitors to listen and dance to music, watch acrobatic performances, watch films and engage in various activities with an XR theme.[207]

Making XR a mass movement led to the founding of multiple branches worldwide and encouraging participation of teenagers in artivism. "We'll hand-paint banners and make sure they're as sharp as possible, thinking about how this might look in photographs, […] the odd drip looks really good."[208] Artivism as group bonding, self-expression, moral intervention, political protest and art project makes XR action exciting for teenagers. Alejandro

Vasquez (aged 18), one member of XR Youth in New York City, explained the appeal of direct action:

> I'm one of the action coordinators, so I've been thinking non-stop about how we can make stuff more creative and more polarizing, so it engages creativity but you also have to put in escalated actions. I feel that's one key component that I love about XR. It challenges me. For example, I'm walking around the City and I'm like, "Oh right there could be an action". And I'm there for the next half hour taking pictures. I'm always scoping out places now just in my regular day to day life.
>
> So we have different degrees of risk taking in actions. Some are not arrestable, like swarming. Like when you take over a road at the crosswalks and do a soft block. A soft block is we're not chained or anything, we're just using our bodies—like linking arms—and we stay until the cops show up and then we go to another place. The whole purpose is to create a gridlock and disrupt business as usual. And then we have actions that are full shutdowns of places or takeovers of areas like we when we took over Times Square. We had a big boat and we kind of put it right in the middle of the intersection and one of our 16 year olds glued himself to the boat and waited. He was the last to get arrested, and we took over Times Square for two plus hours.[209]

Vasquez was motivated by the dire warnings of XR:

> I was at an event for XR adults and you're sitting and Roger Hallam [...] was talking and he went really deep into Extinction Rebellion and saying we're going to be extinct if we don't do anything; large cities will face starvation if we continue doing these things and we don't have enough infrastructure for agriculture in local places, like NYC, which is a food desert, to continue when other places are going to suffer and go through mass migrations, and I remember I had to step back a little bit and like breathe, and then go back in cos it was all serious for three hours...[210]

The composition of XR demonstrators is demographically indistinguishable from the managerial elite. A university study of British XR protestors revealed they are overwhelmingly middle class, highly educated and southern, with an unusually broad range of ages, with more women than men. Of the adults, 85% are educated to degree level. XR supporters are "more likely to be new to protesting than other environmental activists". In the April 2019 protests, 10% of demonstrators were first-time activists, "twice the proportion of 'novices' at climate marches a decade before".[211]

Like many revolutionary groups, XR receives the support of the elite class. In addition to crowdfunding, XR has received large donations from the Kennedys,[212] Gettys,[213] billionaires[214] and charities. It publicly thanked a toiletries manufacturer for a donation.[215] In 2018, a foundation with a history of backing "radical and far left initiatives was created by the German-Greek philanthropist Antonis Schwarz" made a substantial donation to Rising Up! This money was apparently used as start-up capital for XR.[216] £121,140 was donated to XR by Children's Investment Fund Foundation ("the world's largest philanthropy that focuses specifically on improving children's lives") on 8 April 2019.[217]

Rising Up! and XR propose environmental sustainability through restricting capitalism and replacing parliamentary democracy with rulership guided by scientists. Taming free-market capitalism, curbing the unpredictability of democracy (however limited), governance by experts and reducing personal freedom in a system of surveillance, nudge and control—all in the name of environmental sustainability—are goals of super-wealthy globalists, international firms, NGOs and civil servants: Burnham's managerial elite. From the point of view of the big financial backers of XR, its radical proposals act as assault against obstacles the managerial elite faces in its drive towards meshing state and mega-corporations in a top-down managed economy. No conspiracy is needed; it is a natural alignment of interests. For its own ends, the elite opportunistically appropriates the opportunity that XR presents. XR and its supporters are genuinely worried about the environment; big donors feel they are doing their bit for a good cause; policemen do not want to behave toughly towards middle-aged women chained to the doors of banks, and so on. Everyone acts in good faith and with the best of intentions and the slide towards authoritarianism is accelerated.

Etzioni-Halevy explains how elites absorb protest movements: "The aim and/or result of the mechanism is not to eliminate the movement and its activities, or even to alter it completely, but rather to let it persist while dissipating its threat; the aim is to eliminate not the movement itself, but its destabilizing potential. […] This cannot be done in a straightforward manner."[218] C.A. Bond describes how peripheral groups are used by the establishment to undermine sources of competing authority.[219] For a Neo-Marxist analysis of an analogous process, consider the writings of the Critical Theorists on the commodification of avant-garde culture.

XR is an ideal example of a supposedly subversive movement that aligns with the values of the managerial elite's institutions,[220] agencies, charities, think-tanks and governments, all of which seek to limit the population's consumption of resources.[221] XR is used to advance ideas that are the basis of a potential global reset to protect the environment, inaugurating technocracy. At which point, XR becomes disposable.

Four
Institutions & Artivism

The impact of artivism and cultural entryism in the fine arts has been established. This chapter will give more examples. Institutions tend to drift leftward and also tend to expand their remit and power; this phenomenon encourages adoption of artivism by institutions. Initially, it may appear battles over historic statues and heritage organisations are unrelated to artivism. However, resentment at serving a conservative audience is common to all elite administrators of public arts. This resentment fuels support for artivism and demeaning historical material.

Trouble at the top

One art historian suggests administrative instability in the British public arts began under a Conservative government:

> "Change" is to me a neutral term and I am deeply suspicious of politicians and others who promise "change" rather than "improvement". I have the impression that both major British political parties like to present themselves as "radicals", that is to say reformers who are prepared to uproot and alter established practices. The results of this tendency can be good, but in the case of museums and libraries, which have to pursue policies for the longer term, they can be disastrous. There used to be an understanding that the Government ministry concerned with National Museums maintained an "arms-length"

relationship with them. In the case of the V&A this attitude was weakened by the 1983 National Heritage Act under which, at the instance of Margaret Thatcher, a rather powerless Advisory Council was replaced by a Board of Trustees, all of whom, with their Chairman, are appointed by the Prime Minister of the day. In practice Prime Ministers take advice, but the results are unpredictable and not always wise. It is my impression that political pressure has so far been generalised with a bias towards appointing Directors who promise "Change".[222]

It is also worth noting that the director of the Victoria & Albert Museum is Tristram Hunt, former Labour MP, who has used his influence to advance decolonisation of the museum.[223]

This change to a more utilitarian attitude towards heritage saw heritage become a matter of governmental management of assets and maximising tourism revenue. By 2017, governance of heritage had been combined into a department with jurisdiction over heritage, arts, culture, libraries, architecture, royal sites, media, broadcasting, publishing, sport, digital information/media, cyber security, telecommunications, National Archives, national ceremonies, gambling, lottery funding, horse racing, tourism, social action and "loneliness". By late 2021, 10 different ministers had successively held the position of Secretary of State in an 11-year period, with only one change of government during that period. (Over the last 30 years, culture secretaries have had ministerial tenures of an average of 19 months apiece.) A lack of stability and continuity even within the lifespans of governments has rendered the DCMS incompetent, rudderless and in no position to combat the incessant push for change in institutions. Indeed, change is the only certainty at the top of the UK's culture ministry.

The National Trust

The National Trust (NT) was founded in 1895 to care for properties and locations of historical and cultural importance in

Great Britain. It attracted a mass membership through its work conserving and making accessible sites. The majority of its members are currently majority ethnically white British and middle class. Tim Parker was appointed Chairman of the NT in 2014. This coincided with an increasing tendency of the NT to impose a more political outlook.

A former member of staff described how the NT set targets for photographs of ethnic minorities, LGBT and visibly-disabled visitors at NT properties, to be used for publicity purposes. "Imagery was captured mostly using real visitors, but in the beginning it was almost impossible to find people whom were from ethnic groups, so in order to be more successful, the organisation had to invite people to be models, they used staff and their families who were ethnic, or friends or supporters. Some professional models were also hired at the beginning too. This seemed at odds at the time with their strategy of being 'authentic', but I guess all companies and other institutions and charities are guilty of doing the same."[224] Pressure on the staff responsible "was quite high".[225] "Socio-economic groups were also being targeted for more representation across National Trust images. Nobody could really put their finger on a description for this group however."[226] Initial targets—matching census data—were exceeded, with 30% of visitor photographs in the 2019 NT *Handbook* being ethnic minorities and visibly disabled, an unrealistic exaggeration. The prevalent target culture in terms of demographics was considered by some staff to be detrimental to the NT's core functions.

In response to politicisation of the NT at its top level, a group calling itself Restore Trust was founded. It consisted of ex-staff, members and ex-members of the NT. The group want to prompt the NT to: "Protect (maintain standards of conservation and presentation, protect a 'spirit of place', and preserve history for the enjoyment of future generations), conserve (return to founding principles, emphasize evolution not revolution, care for what unites us, and help us to enjoy the places we love) and listen (hear members' views, recognize volunteer contributions, and respect specialist curators)."[227]

The NT's September 2020 report made much of already known links between the North Atlantic slave trade and NT properties.[228] It seemed that the NT was eager to engage in blame and guilt by association regarding properties it was protecting and promoting. In November 2020, Parker stated that the NT was "committed to anti-racism and to creating a diverse, inclusive and welcoming environment". He declared that BLM was a "human rights movement with no party-political affiliation", despite the group's close ties to the Democrat Party and its endorsement of left-wing politics.[229] Following the tabling of a no-confidence motion in the Chairman, Parker resigned in May 2021, leaving office in October 2021.

The Museums Association

The Museums Association (MA) was founded in London in 1889. It is an association for professionals in the museum field and is concerned with best practice and ethics for staff and institutions. It arranges training and seminars and publishes a journal for members.

Like the ICA, the MA has Registered Charity status.[230] The MA is funded by ACE, the Paul Hamlyn Foundation and the Esmée Fairbairn Foundation, which is "committed to social justice, and to tackling injustice and inequality. Racial justice is a critical element in this, in the UK and across the world, and we are committed to addressing structural and systemic racism in the UK both as an organisation and through the work we support."[231] The MA sees no division between this goal and its own. "We are a dynamic membership organisation that campaigns for socially engaged museums and a representative workforce. We work ethically and sustainably and collaborate with partners where we have common aims and values."[232] The MA slogan is "Inspiring museums to change lives". Keynote panel discussions for its 2021 conference were: "We are all complicit in systemic oppression: What can a museum worker do?", "Embedding anti-racism in cultural arts organisations" and "Re-imagining museums for climate action".[233]

Its stress on innovation and openness to new ways of managing museums leaves the MA open to entryism. The MA is one of the driving forces behind the politicisation of museums in the UK, the push to decolonise collections and moves to legalise widespread deaccessioning of cultural patrimony: "We unreservedly support initiatives to decolonise museums and their collections."[234] It offers support to staff wishing to decolonise their institution. It does not state anywhere that there are legitimate grounds against wholesale revision of collections and practices nor does it offer a defence of the universalist principles of the Enlightenment museum. It accepts "climate emergency" as a subject of concern for museums.

The MA uses its influence to undermine the aspiration towards objectivity (of institutions, staff and practices), retention of items, separation of museums from interested outside parties and treating staff, creators and audience equally regardless of race. It is an avowedly campaigning organisation which seeks to advance progressivism under the guise of professional advice to museum staff.[235]

The Association for Art History is in lockstep with the MA: "We strive to reach broad audiences within the UK and those from areas beyond our traditional spheres of scholarship, readership and involvement. We work to reduce barriers to engagement with art history that may exist as a result of economic or social strata, location, age, capacity, race or ethnicity, gender or sexual orientation."[236] The AAH's 2021 festival had many talks specifically devoted to race, immigration, colonialism and multiculturalism. Of named speakers, 29 were female and seven were men.[237] It is almost impossible to find men in the images used as publicity for MA press releases. The political stance of these organisations could not be more overt.

Redefining museums

The International Council of Museums (ICOM) adopted on 24 August 2007 the following definition of a "museum": "A museum is a non-profit, permanent institution in the service of society and its development, open to the public, which acquires, conserves, researches, communicates and exhibits the tangible and intangible heritage of humanity and its environment for the purposes of education, study and enjoyment."[238]

In 2019, ICOM proposed a new definition:

> Museums are democratising, inclusive and polyphonic spaces for critical dialogue about the pasts and the futures. Acknowledging and addressing the conflicts and challenges of the present, they hold artefacts and specimens in trust for society, safeguard diverse memories for future generations and guarantee equal rights and equal access to heritage for all people. Museums are not for profit. They are participatory and transparent, and work in active partnership with and for diverse communities to collect, preserve, research, interpret, exhibit, and enhance understandings of the world, aiming to contribute to human dignity and social justice, global equality and planetary wellbeing.[239]

The old definition allowed no room for political direction. The new definition not only enables curator activism, it mandates it. That is why it has been drafted in that manner. The new definition requires museum staff to act politically. If their collections are insufficiently demographically "inclusive", they must diversify to meet the commitment to inclusion and diversity. "Spaces" turns museums from buildings, collections and staff into flexible abstractions, allowing use of resources for social projects. Social activists will have abolished the museum as we know it and replaced with an unconstrained charter for political action.

That new definition was rejected by francophone museums and has (at time of publication) been returned to the consultation stage. ICOM's board still supports the new definition. Tonya Nelson (London Director of ACE, Trustee of the National Gallery,

London) supports the new definition. Writing for the MA, Nelson suggested only one cosmetic change: "I think 'polyphonic' should be changed to 'many voices', if we want to be seen as accessible and inclusive."[240]

Artivism from academia

Today, universities teach artivism and academics take on the cachet of artists without knowing manual craft skills. To promote the practice and theory of artivism, university galleries act as laboratories for artivist academics and curators. Both Manchester University and Goldsmiths, University of London (formerly Goldsmiths College) have galleries. Universities and venues cross-validate each other.[241]

Art collective Forensic Architecture (FA) (led by Goldsmiths academics) sparked a legal protest in Manchester in the summer of 2021. *Cloud Studies*, an exhibition by FA at Whitworth Museum (part of Manchester University) included data regarding pollution caused by use of tear gas and explosions deployed by Israeli security forces. "[… T]he exhibition *Cloud Studies* features archival material, including maps, 3D printed models and contextual interpretive material related to the methodologies used by FA in their work, and runs from 2 July–17 October 2021."[242] FA presented their documentation to guide conversations regarding a social issue on which they had little forensic detachment. *The Art Newspaper* reported:

> An introductory text to a film in the exhibition begins: "Forensic Architecture stands with Palestine" and continues to outline experiences of "ethnic cleansing" of Palestinian neighbourhoods by "Israeli police and settlers". It continues stating that the Palestinian liberation struggle "is inseparable from other global struggles against racism, white supremacy anti-semitism, and settler colonial violence".[243]

The pressure group UK Lawyers for Israel complained to Manchester University, claiming the exhibition seemed "designed to provoke racial discord". The Jewish legal group also noted that

Eyal Weizman, one of FA's founders, is banned from travelling to the USA "on security grounds".[244] The Whitworth responded to the group's complaints by announcing that it took seriously its duty to avoid supporting racism. The Whitworth had previously been forced to remove a statement supporting Palestine. The anti-Israel, pro-Palestine position is an article of faith on the left. British curators consider the Israel-Palestine issue settled in terms of morality; it would not have occurred to staff at the Whitworth that any visitor might find *Cloud Studies* contentious.

Goldsmiths stated *Cloud Studies* "reflect[s] the Whitworth's commitment to platforming the role of art as a means of social change [...]".[245] The Whitworth had already declared its willingness to make itself a platform for artivism. Director Alistair Hudson commented on FA, "I'm particularly keen on arts-like practice that goes beyond art, that goes beyond the realm of the gallery and the museum..."[246] Manchester University, Goldsmiths, the Whitworth, FA and artivist foundations all share a conviction that art venues are platforms for political activity and there is a settled narrative regarding the Israeli-Palestinian conflict. That the network of individuals shared a single outlook is a demonstration of elitist monoculture in the arts. It also reveals the high level of cross-organisation, funding and sympathetic contact between parties.[247]

The Turner Prize

The Turner Prize is the premier prize for contemporary art in the UK. Founded in 1984, hosted by the Tate and broadcast by Channel 4 Television, it had a high reputation and formerly generated much debate about art in the mass media. It originally rewarded recognised artists of stature, such as winners Howard Hodgkin and Malcolm Morley and nominees Lucian Freud, Paula Rego and Patrick Caulfield. Later, well-known sculptors Anthony Gormley, Rachel Whiteread and Damien Hirst were awarded the prize. While the art was not traditional and drew criticism because of avant-garde techniques, it met the remit of promoting new serious art and stimulating public interest and art criticism.

However, starting in the 2000s, nominations and winners were apparently selected mainly on criteria of politics or demographic characteristics. Thereafter, there was a move away from art that had a strong pictorial (or even visual) character and content. Films, wall texts, computer-image presentations, installations, performances, sound art, architectural displays and documentation of off-site projects were all nominated. Increasingly featured was conceptual art, wherein the physical component of a display is subordinate to the artist's act of nomination and verbal narrative. Artist names were less recognisable; the art had a deliberate amnesiac quality—it was non-visual, indistinct, idea-based, intentionally self-effacing and forgettable.[248] While nominees and winners from early years had gone on to leave a mark in the public consciousness, in later years virtually no Turner Prize artists did.

By the 2000s, the Turner Prize was a shadow of its former self, with the quality of art low and public interest waning.[249] This directly correlated to the foregrounding of material that lacked distinct aesthetic content. Mark Wallinger's *State Britain* (2007)—a collection of placards and material used by a political protester, who had displayed them outside the Houses of Parliament—won the 2007 Turner Prize. In 2015, an art collective called Assemble won the prize. It is a group of architects who frame their activity as art. They won for a community project in Liverpool (Alistair Hudson was part of the jury).[250] This was an indication of the rise of collectives.

Socially-engaged practice is defined by the Tate as follows:

> Socially engaged practice, also referred to as social practice or socially engaged art, can include any artform which involves people and communities in debate, collaboration or social interaction. This can often be organised as the result of an outreach or education program, but many independent artists also use it within their work. The term new genre public art, coined by Suzanne Lacy, is also a form of socially engaged practise. The participatory element of socially engaged practice, is key, with the artworks created often holding equal

or less importance to the collaborative act of creating them. As Tom Finkelpearl outlines in his book What We Made: Conversations on Art and Social Cooperation, social practice is "art that's socially engaged, where the social interaction is at some level the art."[251]

The Tate describes Assemble's Turner Prize-winning activity as "a perfect example of artists using socially engaged practise because they collaborate with residents to improve their local area".[252]

The 2019 prize was shared by four nominees, when they refused to accept hierarchy in art. The 2020 prize was cancelled due to the government-imposed Covid-19 lockdown. Instead, grants were given to artists and collectives; decisions were made on the basis of identity politics. Tate's own summaries of recipients formed a humiliatingly derivative list of ethnicities, sexual orientations and preferred pronouns. The 2021 shortlist included only artivist collectives. The groups were Array Collective, Black Obsidian Sound System (B.O.S.S.), Cooking Sections, Gentle/Radical and Project Art Works.

Array Collective is a group of artists who work in a Belfast studio "who join together to create collaborative actions in response to the sociopolitical issues affecting Northern Ireland".[253] They are all practitioners of new media, environmental art, digital art, online events and community projects, particularly social justice and feminism. "[London-based] Black Obsidian Sound System (B.O.S.S.) formed by and for QTIBPOC (Queer, Trans and Intersex Black and People of Colour), B.O.S.S. challenges the dominant norms of sound-system culture across the African diaspora through club nights, art installations, technical workshops and creative commissions." "Cooking Sections is a London-based duo examining the systems that organise the world through food. Using site-responsive installation, performance and video, they explore the overlapping boundaries between art, architecture, ecology and geopolitics."[254] Cardiff's Gentle/Radical describes their activity as: "Our activities shift according to cultural need, interest, and the challenges our communities are facing. [...] We create projects that work across different communities, art forms and spaces. […] Whilst we're interested in 'art' and 'culture', we don't see creativity as exclusive to these spheres."[255] Hastings-based Project Art Works is "a collective of neurodiverse artists and activists. Our programmes evolve through creative practice and radiate out to awareness raising in the cultural and care sectors, promoting more diverse representation in programming and relevancy for audiences."[256]

However worthwhile the groups' activities are—as therapy, community work, social outreach, education and advocacy—they are all ancillary to fine-art making and therefore ineligible for a fine-art award. Tate sees its duty to act as a social organisation by appropriating the ethos of artivists. B.O.S.S. was quick to criticise this appropriation of their work by the British arts establishment —led by anxious, middle-class, left-wing, self-hating (overwhelmingly white) university graduates—who use minorities as political tokens and shields to bolster their organisation's status and government income. Following nomination, B.O.S.S. stated: "The urgency with which we have been asked to participate, perform and deliver demonstrates the extractive and exploitative practices in prize culture, and more widely across the industry […] We understand that we are being instrumentalized […]"[257] B.O.S.S. bemoaned a "lack of adequate financial remuneration for collectives in commissioning budgets and artist fees, and in the industry's in-built reverence for individual inspiration over the diffusion, complexity and opacity of collaborative endeavour".[258] It was a demand for more resources, directed (one assumes) to recipients congenial to B.O.S.S.'s outlook; the language and demands are indistinguishable from those of a pressure group.

By 2021, the logical impetuses of the Turner Prize organisers (to blur the line between art and politics, to seek greater social relevance in a time of diminishing public interest) and artivists (to claim more public-arts resources) had reached a natural conclusion: the Turner Prize would no longer be an art prize but an artivism award.[259]

Summary

Institutions are high-status targets for entryism, not least because of the disproportionate influence of the public sector. Over the course of decades, the cultural sector has become dominated by the state, which champions principles and incentives that lock administrators into a cycle of accelerating utilitarianism. The arts-administrator class, which is approaching a political monoculture, lacks advocates of connoisseurship and the art-for-art's-sake principle. Within the public arts, there are too many vested interests for the formation of effective resistance against artivism.

Case Study

Stuckists as Anti-Artivists

The Stuckist movement was founded in London in 1999 by artists Billy Childish (b. 1959) and Charles Thomson (b. 1953) in opposition to institutional and mass-media support for the Young British Artist (YBA) group. The art of the YBAs was collected, exhibited, promoted and traded by collector and advertising mogul Charles Saatchi. It was Saatchi who grouped these artists under the school — or brand — of "the YBAs". The mixture of highbrow arts coverage, tabloid-press outrage and exposure in multiple public venues led to commercial success and widespread recognition. The Saatchi collection of YBA art was exhibited at the *Sensation* exhibition at the Royal Academy, London, in 1997. YBA art was collected by the Government Art Collection and promoted overseas by the British Council. The Stuckist movement was named after the gibe of Tracey Emin (a leading YBA) who accused painter Childish of "being stuck".

Issued on 4 August 1999, the Stuckist manifesto declared, "Artists who don't paint aren't artists. [...] Post-Modernism, in its adolescent attempt to ape the clever and witty in modern art, has shown itself to be lost in a cul-de-sac of idiocy. What was once a searching and provocative process (as Dadaism) has given way to trite cleverness for commercial exploitation."[260] The authors condemned novelty and art-school system as "a slick bureaucracy, whose primary motivation is financial".[261] They identified institutional support in the rise of YBA art, which sometimes appropriated or plagiarised other art.[262] "Brit Art, in being sponsored by Saatchis, mainstream conservatism and the Labour government, makes a mockery of its claim to be subversive or avant-garde." Stuckists do not espouse a unified style but a common purpose within a set of positive and negative positions.

The Stuckists — by then enlarged to include more disaffected artists — staged a protest outside the Tate Gallery during the 2000 Turner Prize display, something that was repeated at subsequent exhibitions. Although Stuckists engage in demonstrations, they do not claim these as art. Quite the contrary; they are resolutely in favour of the definition of fine art being restricted to the normal categories. Their action was both artivist (in that they were actively intervening in an art event, acting as artists) and anti-artivist (in that they were protesting against dilution of resources and attention received in the fine-art field due to the influx of what they considered non-art material). They staged their own group exhibition (*The Real Turner Prize Show*, Pure Gallery, London, 2000). The Stuckists have opposed the self-serving network of leading galleries, major collectors and public art institutions at the top of the British art world. Thomson exposed the conflict of interest apparent in the purchase of a suite of paintings by Chris Ofili by the Tate Gallery, while he served as trustee on its board. The high price paid for these paintings was robustly challenged by experts.

The Stuckists have expanded to dozens of affiliated groups of artists worldwide, all working in conventional materials and disavowing conceptual, new-media and performance art forms. In groups and individually, British Stuckists have exhibited widely but there has only been one academic symposium and exhibition held in a major museum (Liverpool, 2004). No Stuckist has become as widely celebrated as the YBAs. From the outside, it appears that, when Stuckists presented an objection to establishment-sanctioned conceptual art, they were ostracised by British museums. One conclusion could be that when dissenting artists (by no means firm traditionalists) attack the *idées fixes* of art establishment and art market, they are marginalised and ignored, in sharp contrast to the politically useful activities of avant-gardists and artivists, whose activities are funded and promoted.

Here are Thomson's thoughts on artivism:

> There is effectively nothing that cannot be conscripted as art, if someone chooses to do it. It is not the object or activity in itself that can achieve this. It is the status of the denoter, their respect and power within the art world. The press are only too eager to give publicity when a person or body deemed to be authoritative in the arts does something which is widely considered among the public to be ludicrous. The exponents of a self-defined radical arts caucus are only too glad in return to consider their position reinforced as being at odds with a philistine public and rely on historical precedent, where all the art movements of modernism have been initially reviled and later revered. There is however a significant difference between now and then which seems to have escaped today's art establishment. It was not just the public who jeered at the Impressionists, the Cubists et al. There was not at the time a divide between the public and the art establishment. It was also the art establishment doing the jeering and it was also the art establishment whose conventional taste was proved wrong. This is exactly the same today. How can it be anything other than conventional if it is automatically lauded by the art establishment?
>
> I have had direct experience—quite against my intention—of enacting artivism of the other definition, namely something not previously considered art but being redefined as art. On the surface, my activity has all the requirements and is begging to be labelled art, but I choose not to do so. It was a demonstration. It was actually one of a number of demonstrations, held annually (sometimes bi-annually) over a 20-year period. It was staged mainly by artists (particularly from an art movement, the Stuckists) against an art prize (the Turner Prize), outside an art gallery (Tate Britain) and even involved varied visual props and costumes. I could of course have

easily announced that the demonstrations were art. However, I chose not to, although I had the fantasy of the demonstrations being nominated for the Turner Prize, so our demonstration could be inside as part of the Prize, while we were simultaneously demonstrating against it outside, but the Tate as usual missed a trick here. Another year, we displayed (imitation) skulls on top of a row of posts with the slogan on placards that they had died of boredom from the Turner Prize.

Activism in general is accurately defined by that word and likewise demonstrations by the word I've just used. But there seems to be a fetish nowadays to conflate everything with the term art, as if that somehow gives it a greater status — probably because it does give that impression. After all, art has been revered down the centuries and that lustre accompanies the term, however inappropriately it might be used. Art is a term that needs to be retained and applied to activities whose primary function is artistic, not to activities which incorporate an artistic element (or even the participation of artists), but whose obvious intent is something completely different to creating a work of art. A work of art with a message is an entirely different animal to a message which makes use of the techniques of art.[263]

Stuckist painter Ella Guru observed, "A soup kitchen is a good thing in general as it feeds people. But how is that 'art'? As a Stuckist I would say it's not art. It's a community service. A soup kitchen as art is as ridiculous as a crumpled ball of paper on a plinth being called 'art'. Stuckism was started as a reaction against such absurd items (a glass of water on a shelf; pickled sharks; unmade beds) being called art and that I still agree with. As for the political content of Stuckist works, that depends on the artist."[264]

In his essay "Reclaiming Art as a Force for Liberty", American Stuckist Richard Bledsoe suggests how artivism became so favoured:

The main reason the awkward word and practice of artivism is gaining traction in the alienated modern art world (and nowhere else) is that substituting propaganda for art fulfills the globalist agenda. Like a tainted Midas, everything leftism touches turns into witless and bullying collectivist policy statements. The totalitarian impulse for control demands that all means serve statist ends; artivism is part of that mindset. The Cultural Marxists embedded in our institutions make sure this is the kind of art that gets support, attention, and funding. […]

That kind of mentoring takes money. Their website reveals that one of the entities pulling the puppet strings is the Open Society Foundations, one of George Soros's money-laundering fronts. It's no accident that this enemy of liberty puts artists on the payroll to inject toxic messaging into society. Another supporter is the National Endowment for the Arts. Our own government is funding the subversion and perversion of the culture. But whom is this ultimately benefiting? […]

The governing philosophy of would-be overlords worldwide is Postmodernism. The Postmodern mindset believes that reality is formed by the manipulation of language, in the service of the preferences of the powerful. The globalist governing elites have constructed a simulated world where their customs of sophistry, networking, and bureaucratic manoeuvring dominate. […]

Traditionally, art has shown us who we are, and what we can be, in ways almost impossible to reduce into language. True art delivers the inspiration to live up to ideals. True art gives the encouragement to think and feel deeply. True art causes a yearning to harmonize with truth and beauty. The politicized hacks of the modern art world can't produce profound insights, so they lie about what art is and what it is for. This vital means of communication was hijacked, its function betrayed. But we still hunger for the real thing. We need it. […]

We must fight back against these attempts to destroy us from within. Let art become one of our weapons. It's a counterattack the Marxists will never see coming because they assume that's already thoroughly conquered territory. From an institutional standpoint, they are correct. [...] Renew the arts, and renew the civilization.[265]

Critic Edward Lucie-Smith (who has been supportive of some Stuckists) sees an opportunity for alternative art scenes to emerge in the near future:

> It is I think clear that there's going to be a great shake up in the British art world as the [Covid] epidemic diminishes. It's clear that it won't fade away completely, and may in future always be a factor. [...] Serota-ist[266] "art for the people" is a lot more complicated than it used to be, both in present circumstances, and probably also in the immediately foreseeable future. Basically, the blah-blah about art presented democratically to the people was based on a lie. The pitch was that these big exhibitions of the latest contemporary art were for eager young audiences — 18-to-35-year-olds, preferably those living in London or very close to it. [...] On weekdays, most of the mass audience the official galleries were looking for and indeed getting were tourists. Tate Modern as an alternative to visiting the Tower of London. [...] Those troops of spectators have vanished.[267]

Once the mass audience for art is reduced, Lucie-Smith considers major museums may have to reconsider priorities.

It is impossible to make an artistic assessment of a group as diverse as the Stuckists as an art movement. Even taking an overall view of Stuckism outside of collective statements is difficult. We can say that the Stuckist movement acts as a concerted opposition to conceptual art, the excesses of performance art and instrumentalist use of art by the state. It is the closest thing to a dissident movement in art today and, consequently, it has been dismissed or ignored by critics and arts administrators. This establishment disapproval and the fact that it has attracted a large number of artist supporters suggest Stuckism is an authentic anti-artivist art movement.

Five

The Business of Artivism

Artivism is a staple of art biennales and cultural festivals and a component of museum programming. Publishers and authors capitalise on artivism; academics make artivism a locus of study and participate in art collectives. Artivism is embedded in museums, academia, commerce and publishing just as deeply as it is within social movements.

Universities and the Center for Artistic Activism

There are many instances of legal-pressure groups and activist law professors turning to art, as already encountered in the case of Forensic Architecture (FA). Universities such North Carolina[268] and Texas[269] include courses on artivism. (With the University of Texas at Austin promoting the work of Julio Salgado—a self-declared illegal immigrant and activist.[270]) The University of Wisconsin offers artivism as an extra-curricular activity.[271] One of the artivism course leaders at Adelphi University, New York, is director of the university's criminal justice programme[272] and there are common references to artivism being an arm of criminal reform, justice action and community resistance to unfair policing and courts. As Adelphi University puts it: "The mission of this interdisciplinary, multi-institutional collaboration is to engage people in changing society through the power of art."[273] Helguera notes, "[…] art students attracted to this form of art-making often find themselves wondering whether it would be more useful to abandon art altogether and instead become professional community organizers, activists, politicians, ethnographers, or sociologists."[274]

Following the lead of FA at Goldsmiths, the artivism multi-disciplinary research group was established at John Moores Liverpool University. The group's aim is to:

> engage with marginalised communities through methodologies that place participants at the centre of the creative process. At the heart of this approach is our desire to work at the intersections of social policy, cultural studies, politics, and social theory by providing a platform with political currency. The Artivism Research Group is a team of multidisciplinary researchers who are seeking to explore the potential of artivism for criminological inquiry. By bringing criminologists and artists together the group seeks to develop a programme of collaborative work considering "artivism" as a means to effect social change.[275]

Such blending of knowledge and guidance in public-policy matters relates closely to experts using "nudge" policies to implement change secretly and without consultation.[276] There is more than one academic paper to be written about interrelations of nudge policy, public-relations management and artivism.

The Center for Artistic Activism (CAA) was founded in New York City in 2009.[277] The directors are Rebecca Bray (ex-Smithsonian) and Steve Lambert ("artistic activist"); it was co-founded by Lambert and Steve Dunmore (sociology lecturer). It offers what one would expect from an art school or university: courses, webinars, lectures, workshops, publications, mobile-phone apps and podcasts. It researches artivism and provides grants to practitioners. Its goals are expressly progressive. One of the art designs on the CAA website says "migration is beautiful".

It arranges projects and works with partners to implement social change. CAA operates a consultancy service. Its donors include the David Rockefeller Foundation, Open Society Foundations and the NEA. It has worked with the Metropolitan Museum, Greenpeace, the Public Defender Association, Yes Lab,[278] Intelligent Mischief[279] and Beautiful Trouble.[280] These donors and partners are involved in street activism, new-media presence, legal advocacy, political lobbying, creative consultancy and public relations, all allied in progressivism. The money circulating comes from corporations wishing to improve their images, pressure groups wishing to make an impact, charities needing to disburse sums periodically and state agencies with annual budgets to be allocated. CAA has worked in "19 countries, on 4 continents", participating in art events, many state funded. The website encourages artivists to disrupt official meetings. "Government meetings can become a key performance venue with some clever planning. The bar is already set so low that one can easily say their peace [sic] and do it with panache!"

Just as artivism is cover for lobbying, so artivism also justifies criminality:

> [...] adding or subordinating the category of art to that of typical activism provides a valuable trump-card when artivists come to defend themselves against the authorities. When you defend that what you're doing is an art form or a cultural contribution to the city, it's accepted without a fuss. When Manuel Delgado Ruiz argued in court that he'd set fire to a container to create an art work, the case was shelved. When art is put into the equation the authorities and political bigwigs no longer feel threatened. The label of "art" provides clever camouflage for the fierce will to struggle.[281]

Las Agencias made clothing items to facilitate shoplifting: "For Las Agencias, shoplifting is a type of civil disobedience in which reflexive kleptomania is directed against the homogenizing and instrumentalizing effect of global capital."[282] Raising money for bail bonds is a commonplace activity: "Mickey Melendez is part of the New York's Young Lords, which is a Latino liberationist direct action group. He talks about the dancing and performances by Tito Puente at fundraisers to raise money to pay for lawyers to keep activists out of jail and the music during meetings."[283]

In a postmodernist era, there is no threshold for competence or content. Any activity can be nominated as art. Just as any art (or non-art) can be admitted to an art venue, it is conversely not possible to argue that any particular activity or material has no place in an art venue. Aesthetics is no longer a legitimate test of quality.[284] Consider the view of Lucy Lippard, doyenne of the feminist art movement: "[…] 'quality' — that elusive bailiwick for the conservative wing of the art-for-art's crowd."[285] Whitney Chadwick, leading feminist art historian: "In the face of protests by blacks, students, and women, the fiction of an art world isolated from broader social and political issues by 'objectivity,' 'quality,' and 'aesthetics' began to be exposed."[286] The idea of qualitative appreciation of art — the very essence of discrimination — is treated with disdain; it is reduced to a notional concept or a shield for reactionaries fighting a rear-guard action against the massed allies of progressivism.

In contemporary art criticism, visual appearance is of little relevance because the focus is upon ideas, identity and context. This has effectively disarmed both traditionalists and modernists, who hold that the content of art resides in its visual appearance. The field is ceded to postmodernists, who see the arts as an interplay of concepts, dematerialised, in a zone of semantic flux and competing interests. Far from being a dissection of hierarchy, postmodernism permits might-is-right as an effective strategy for excluding unfavoured art, invalidating criticism and delegitimatizing opponents. Without having to consider consensus, tradition, usual criteria or informed critiques, postmodernist-supporting administrators present art and artivism in terms of uplifting the marginalised and challenging oppressive norms in ways that seem compassionate and openminded; yet all the time, they engage in ruthless realpolitik derived from hegemony which allows the elite to exclude art it dislikes, advance favoured narratives and patronise certain producers, all without engaging in debate.

Charities advancing artivism

The Ford Foundation uses its $12.4bn endowment to support artivism and political causes. That money that would have gone to community projects and social work (rather than to fine art) had it not gone to artivism. Yet there is evidence that money that would otherwise have gone to fine art is being diverted to artivism. In May 2021, the Tate announced its (previously discussed) list of artist collectives for the Turner Prize. In August 2021, the Serpentine Gallery, London, divided £100,000 between "10 London-based artists and collectives, working at the intersection of art, spatial politics and community practice".[287] Aside from McArthur Fellowships of $625,000 over five years, there is the Jane Lombard Prize for Art and Social Justice, worth $25,000. Freelands Foundation gave £3m in diversity grants in 2020. Art for Justice is an American non-profit organisation which supports leftist political causes and seeks to promote these through art. It has $100m founding capital. It describes payments as "advocacy grants".[288] Another activist foundation is The Paul Hamlyn Foundation, which supports art that allows individuals to "overcome disadvantage and lack of opportunity".[289] Financial data shows that foundation funds are disbursed to pro-migration advocacy organisations unconnected to the arts. The Freelands Foundation publishes reports ascribing underperformance of women artists to systemic sexism. The foundation—like many other foundations—is a lobbying group. It runs an award that funds exhibitions only by women. The South London Gallery received £136,000 from the Freelands Trust.[290] The 2019 and 2020 programme of that public art museum consisted of solo exhibitions by nine female and two male artists. Whether a lobbying organisation is (before or after the fact) financing a public venue disproportionately favouring women is a moot point; the result is the same. The founder and chairwoman of Freelands is Elisabeth Murdoch, daughter of Rupert Murdoch. Elisabeth Murdoch is Chairman [*sic*] of the Tate Modern Advisory Council; Freelands also donates to the Tate.[291] The Tate is led by feminist Maria Balshaw. The largest British art prize is Artes

Mundi, a politically determined biennial award given to conceptual, new-media or artivism artists.

The June 2019 issue of the Museums Association newsletter contained a text by Alistair Hudson, Director of Manchester City and Whitworth Galleries (already mention in relation to FA). In it, he explains how a £75,000 grant from two arts-activist organisations, Outset Partners[292] and Arte Util, would be used to alter the museums' missions: "Using a methodology that sees art not as a set of objects, but a process and tool for social change, our museums will radically transform their core protocols by redrawing relationships with local constituent groups, creating an agency to inform the museums' collecting, curating and presenting."[293] This donation came four years after Hudson had given Arte Util a platform at the venue he had managed.[294]

Two of Arte Util's eight stated aims are to "propose new uses for art within society" and "replace authors with initiators and spectators with users".[295] This is code for, respectively, adoption of artivism and establishment of political-art collectives. "Arte Util projects' primary objective remains concrete social transformation", according to an internal report.[296] Hudson's text about payment of money to the Manchester Art Gallery and Whitworth by Outset Partners will be used to "de-modernise" the institutions. The plan is to "reuse our buildings as places to generate conversations between people about what we need to do and what we need to address". The promised move is for museums to partner with "local constituent groups, creating an agency to inform the museums' collecting, curating and presenting". Would it be communities or selected pressure groups making their voices heard? When Hudson writes of "artistic strategies to make change happen", it is clear what type of change he envisages. If communities wanted local museums to celebrate British imperialism, one doubts this suggestion would be entertained. If the local community decided it did not want "conversations between people about what we need to do" but instead a museum that aspired to neutrality and was devoted to presenting the best art, sensitively curated and informatively explained, would that community's wishes be respected?

What sort of community input Hudson expects is evident in his track record. In his previous role as Director of Middlesbrough Institute of Modern Art, Hudson had previously programmed a pro-migrant advocate whose exhibition was entitled "ABC of Racist Europe" and another exhibition was "If All Relations Were to Reach Equilibrium, Then This Building Would Dissolve, [which] explores the tension between free circulation and border control as well as the experience of exile and displacement, and focuses on human rights, governmental policies, xenophobia, identity, and trauma, among other themes". Another artist Hudson programmed was Mexican performance artist Pablo Helguera, who had written a guide on how to practice artivism.[297]

In consultations, some groups and views would be favoured; others would be accorded less consideration. Community involvement can be used as cover for instituting policies close to the hearts of the existing cadre of museum administrators. This apparent diffusion of decision-making responsibility could be interpreted as strategic cover to enable use of museum resources for political campaigns and social activism. Selective consulting is an established tactic used by administrators who cite community engagement.[298] In return for the sham of inclusivity, directors expect to steer consultees towards predestined conclusions. Creation of consultative agencies invites pressure groups and self-appointed community leaders to use museums as platforms for their politics. The volunteer partners Hudson seeks are campaigners. To give these groups formal access to the decision-making process is to invite balkanisation of museums. It is a short road to political activists exploiting the status, funds and assets of art museums for factional gain.[299]

Critical Theory and postmodernism may assert that the idea museums are impartial is a fiction, designed to cover for resource exploitation and hegemonic social structures, but removing the aspiration of political neutrality will dissolve consensual support for public funding of museums. The universal nationwide publicly-funded museum network will not be sustainable if museums become overtly political platforms. Taxpayers will support apolitical art venues (even if they visit irregularly); they will not support political-campaign centres. The community-consultation plan invites iconoclasts into the museum and will — paradoxically — end in the destruction of publicly-funded museums.

Establishment-directed revolutionaries

> The artivist (artist+activist) uses her artistic talents to fight and struggle against injustice and oppression — by any medium necessary. The artivist merges commitment to freedom and justice with the pen, the lens, the brush, the voice, the body, and the imagination.
>
> —M.K. Asante[300]

An essay written by Benjamin Barson and Gizelxanath Rodriguez explains their motivation and (indirectly) the mindset of the artivist:[301] "Not only do we see the ever-present tide of artists fighting racism, oppression, and physical and artistic colonialism, but we see them self-consciously drawing from the wells of their pasts, deploying and redeploying the examples of their adopted ancestors." They are alarmed by "recent dramatic downturns in global health and upticks in global fascism and unhinged capitalism". Seeing the situation as a matter of survival in the face of mass forces, they view themselves as revolutionaries. "But how does one 'be' an Artivist? Is the end objective to address social issues and challenge oppression from the microphone, the stage, or the notated score? We do not profess to have all the answers. But we feel the Artivist must go beyond critiquing the moment in which they were born." They then go on to quote "the great Italian communist Antonio Gramsci". "Artivism is about creating a new culture rooted in the struggles against patriarchal capitalism from time-immemorial. It is where the interconnection between the rejection of the oppressors' mores meets with the quest to construct a new being and a new way of being."

Not only do we see artists fighting apparent racism, oppression and physical and artistic colonialism, but we see them self-consciously drawing from the wells of their heritage by deploying and redeploying examples of their adopted ancestors. An artivist sees herself as a revolutionary in a long line of heroes that she evokes. She is an underdog but not alone. She is part of a network fighting against forces that have retarded the progress of the marginalised since time immemorial. Her struggle is part of a wider story that is being conducted by comrades on many fronts. She is on the right side of history. Her cause will win because it is inevitable. History is irreversible.

It does not occur to an artivist that the institutions she rails against are filled with individuals who believe as she does. It does not seem strange to her that such huge entrenched forces of patriarchy and capitalism seem unable to resist a guerrilla movement of the oppressed and that concessions come regularly in every area, written into law and lavishly funded. Every sign of support she gets from someone who is in a position to assist her cause comes from an embattled renegade rather than from the system itself. Every offer of mediation and consultation — obviously, she decides, devices to confuse and divide progressives — is accompanied by money, recognition and acknowledgement of the moral case of her revolutionary creed. The internal narrative is unshakeable — she is an outsider.[302] In truth, the managerial elite use her cosmopolitanism, multicultural relativism, feminism, social liberalism, atheism and communalist spirit to undermine and destroy traditionalism that provides one of the last vestiges of intransigence for the elite. She is a foot soldier of the ruling class.

Leftists are pleased to point out the way government policies "use art as a distraction from detrimental neoliberal policies, including but not limited to austerity, gentrification, arms dealing, capital flight, tax evasion, environmental disaster and the day-to-day sociocultural and economic consequences of such states of affairs".[303] When it comes to how establishment interests and activist demands align on the topics of state-sponsored artivism, these leftists delude themselves into thinking they are holding the powerful to account. The powerful bask in artivist environments, attend the private views, donate and congratulate themselves at these leftist-led excoriations. One cannot detect a flicker of self-awareness in the thousands of pages of artivist literature.

Artivism supports the causes of "gender and equality, labor rights, acknowledgement of the class struggle, economic disparity, animal rights, […] education reform",[304] "criticism of uncontrolled tourism, respect for animals, political corruption, human rights, citizen security, borders, refugees, feminism",[305] decolonisation, racial injustice, incarceration, human-rights abuse, sexual abuse, domestic abuse, AIDS education, healthcare provision, abortion, childcare provision, indigenous rights, violent crime, immigration, hate speech, policing, nuclear weapons, nuclear power, environmental pollution, sex work, voting access and others. On all of these points, the elite that dominates Western governments, international bodies, major charities and (many) billionaire-funded policy foundations agree with progressives. The elite share the aims of leftists. They differ about speed and means but they readily promote Universal Basic Income (UBI), women's empowerment, mass migration (allied to digital identities and digital currency), restricted speech, lowered religious influence, more universal rights, green energy, reduced consumption, multi-ethnic societies, fractured populations, eroded traditions and greater global interdependence.

Notwithstanding the anti-globalisation tenor of artivism[306] and tracing origins of the current wave of artivism back to WTO Seattle summit (1999) and Occupy Wall Street (2008), artivists' aims are largely congruent with the materialist, internationalist, progressivist character of the leading corporations, banks, charities and NGOs which accelerate globalisation. Supposed revolutionaries are actually the establishment's activist wing.

Embracing the serfdom of UBI

A 2021 press release promoted poetry in inner cities; it was from an organisation called Poet in the City.[307] It advertised four forthcoming events, all of which fell into the categories of socially-engaged art or artivism. The subjects were opposition to borders, state provision of housing and feminism within BLM protest. The fourth was UBI.

> Bringing together the Repeat Beat Poet and Bea Bannister from UBI Labs Youth, this episode will explore Universal Basic Income and what it could mean for young people today. UBI Labs Network & UBI Labs Youth is a decentralised network of citizens, researchers and campaigners exploring the potential of Universal Basic Income. Bea Bannister is a student from North London currently studying for her A-levels. A long term supporter of a Universal Basic Income, Bea is a member of UBI Lab Youth and a co-founder of UBI Lab Women. She is passionate about exploring the vast range of effects a UBI could have on the lives of so many different people.[308]

Artists on the left concerned about poverty turn to the state to sustain them. This is becoming increasingly common. Only recently, the Design and Artists Copyright Society released a report recommending UBI for artists: "DACS is proposing that the Government trials a pilot UBI scheme for recent art graduates to enable them to navigate the first two years post-graduation which are the most precarious and financially challenging, now made even more difficult by the effects of the pandemic."[309] This overlooked the fact that it was the government's restrictions regarding Covid-19 (not the virus) that caused duress. The logic is that, since art is a social good and that artists are very lowly paid, the state should pay subsistence-level income for artists.

The prime reason producers of conceptual art, artivism and derivative paintings remain poor is because the market correctly discerns there is nothing there worth supporting. For the actually talented artists drowned in the dross, it can be frustrating. Many skilled artists never reach an audience in order to be judged because there are too many of them and too few collectors.[310] The problem is not the state's failure to support artists, but the overproduction of artists through subsidised art courses and provision of grants, leading to a glut of artists in a competitive market, causing low artist income. In other words, the main cause of artist poverty is government subsidy.[311]

However, to the average artist of a leftist outlook, who endures poverty and whose art is neglected, the problems seem to be art-as-investment and commodification of art. The state looks to be a steady source of income, with the added bonus that anything can pass as art today. There is no aesthetic competency threshold. This is why UBI appeals. UBI provides a safety net, giving artists enough time to set themselves up in their careers before they can gain income from their production. Like the provisional supports of welfare income, dole, universal credit and unemployment payments, UBI would provide just enough to sustain existence. Once the effort and loss of moving to an alternative non-state source of income is factored in, recipients have an incentive to stay out of employment until a threshold much higher than their benefits is attainable. UBI could provide not a safety net but a sticky spider's web that reduces a subject's will and ability to progress towards independence.

UBI is a danger to general liberty because it ties individuals to the control by the state. The state does not work for the citizen but the reverse. The individual comes to rely on UBI, which is at the discretion of the state. Knowing how authorities seek to micromanage, nudge and incentivise people for their own gain, it is too generous to assume that UBI will not be linked to an ever-growing list of requirements of conduct, speech and thought. Paid in a digital currency (perhaps time-dependent or limited to certain purposes — both of which have been mooted by financial experts) and linked to a digital identity, the subject is now in what is a social-credit system in all but name. He becomes subject to monitoring through more channels, conscious that his income relies on the beneficence of the state. All the while, the subject's known political opinions and his position in the hierarchy of privilege/oppression is recalculated by algorithm, assigning him variable income, social-credit rating and access to resources. How can that be a basis for the production of flourishing, original and probing art? Yet, viewed short term by a failing artist, UBI looks like a solution to poverty. UBI is actually a lure on a hook. The hook is serfdom to the state.

Funnelling minority creators into artivism

Martha Rosler perceptively noted that public funding disproportionately benefits minority-demographics creators.[312] Her point was about iniquity of defunding[313] but it also made an associated point: how minority groups, political collectives and artivists (compared to "more mainstream-oriented artists")[314] rely on state support. It is not that minority artists are any less capable of producing saleable work than any other group or that they have less access to gallerists, competitions or publications. It is that the incentives of producing non-commercial work come from politically directed patronage, be that the state, charities or patrons. Elite liberals (who direct funds) act as protectors and promoters to favoured groups and individuals. This encourages minority producers (who produce in a field which does not impede them engaging in commercial production) to monetise their demographic status in a way not available to majority-population artists. It has been monetised by women artists for a century.[315]

Public funding apportioned by liberals leads to the creation of a field of state-supported minority-artists-as-minorities engaged in artivism. This causes them to neglect production of commercially appealing art. Consequently—neglecting technical skills and market acumen—artivists become dependent upon patronage. It is not so different from the debilitating effect of welfare dependence. Cruelly, this inculcation reduces artivists to subsistence level, robbed of the attributes of competency. Maintaining this anti-capitalist stance requires the support of an advanced capitalist economy with surplus money reallocated through taxation to social goods in a generous and self-critical public-arts system. Without capitalism, artivism would not exist. More generally, protection of state funding for art has become such an article of faith that when an artivist wanted to fabricate outrageous inconceivable topics for spoof academic papers, one of them was the abolition of national arts funding.[316]

Encouragement by university tutors for students to produce political art and disdain commercialism causes new artists impoverishment. Creating an underclass of artists whose livelihoods depend on artivism, charity-funded projects and state subsidies produces pliant potential art workers. Failed artists see UBI as necessary because of their bruising experience in the competitive market. Funnelling minority creators into artivism forms an underclass minority-heavy group. UBI proponents request privileged income for that group because it is poor, the implication being that it is so because of individuals' race/sexuality/ethnicity/etc., not because of external stimuli. This system would create a client group actively propagandising on behalf of UBI, which would develop into a benefits/control system which would both sustain and entrap an underclass of creators.

Artivism for income

In 1988, Coco Fusco (b. 1960) wrote, "Western cultural institutions such as the avant-garde have a history of rejuvenating themselves through the exploitation of disempowered peoples and cultures."[317] In 2020, the ICA promoted her with the following text: "Coco Fusco draws parallels with the early 1990s to make the point that it is not artists who need to change, but rather art institutions that need to learn from them and start applying this knowledge. The text was originally written for the Ford Foundation's Creative Futures series."[318] The Ford Foundation has allocated $150m for artivism. The fantasy of a Cuban-American artist operating as an outsider battling for marginalised people is undercut by a leading British state-funded venue promoting Fusco's receipt of a grant by the world's largest progressive-supporting multi-billion-dollar foundation. In 2021, Fusco was among 15 Latino artists receiving a separate $50,000 payment from a $5m grant from the Ford Foundation, Mellon Foundation and U.S. Latinx Art Forum.[319]

The paradoxicality of supposedly marginalised groups being the greatest recipients of financial, institutional and press support is embedded in the oppositional-artist economy. Artivists take alternating views of their exploitation, sometimes condemning it, sometimes exploiting it, sometimes unaware of how they are being used. Artivists condemn their big-money benefactors even as they receive payments—which they consider (inadequate) reparations.

Fine art is a field within which it is notoriously difficult to make a living income.[320] One survey discovered that the median income for a fine artist in 2010 in the UK was £10,000 (from art), less half the average national income.[321] Many artists of some skill and holding professional qualifications earn much less per annum. Most are forced to seek income from outside the art field. Cross-subsidising through paid work, spousal support or inheritance are widespread. By 2015, the average annual income from art for a British artist fell to roughly £6,020, out of an average total income of £16,500 from all sources. Sixty-nine percent of artists needed paid employment. Thirty-six percent of artists earned a negligible £1,000 or less per annum from their art.[322] In the Netherlands, 40% of artists received no income at all from art.[323] Income can fluctuate wildly for lesser-known artists, depending on opportunities and chance sales. A good year is no predicator of the following year for any artist who has no set exhibition schedule or confirmed commissions. Judged purely upon financial self-sufficiency, experienced qualified artists can flip between professional and amateur status on an annual basis.

Artists with low profiles, uncertain incomes, impaired health, motherhood responsibilities and changing domestic commitments find that artivism—like one-off performances—offers a supplementary income stream and a way of refreshing one's CV. The most flexible artists take up residencies, teach courses abroad or relocate for projects. Rootlessness is a sign not just of cosmopolitan global citizenry; it can be a sign of *anomie* and aimlessness. Rootlessness is a key characteristic of the modern artist.[324] Artists can be passive and opportunistic, notwithstanding their articulate interviews and passionate personal avowals. Artivism seems for many artists the lowest level of engagement as a practising artist, one level above departing the art field completely. It is often the domain of the dilletante, recent graduate or artist in faltering mid-career.

One British artist who achieved minor attention in the late 1990s had, by 1999, started to move into collaborative activity. In 2016, she became a registered midwife and her current activism relates to birth issues and related social topics. Her website promotes her artivism and midwifery but does not feature an exhibition list. Selected images feature her in performances and demonstrations; it has no page dedicated to her fine art.[325] An example of this situation is raised to show how difficult an artist's career can be in a field with more supply than demand, serving a fickle fashion-following public.

We should not (without specific information to the contrary) ascribe any one artist's adoption of artivism to solely contingent and financial causes, although we must consider those possible spurs. In earlier eras, teaching was the most reliable source of supplementary income for artists. Nowadays, with so much competition for tertiary-level art-teaching jobs, artists are forced by necessity to offer a wider range of services, including artivism. Venues and local councils have funds earmarked for artivism — either as social outreach or as part of the general budget — and solicit for such activity. Commissioners apply no artistic assessment to proposed artivist events and artivists are immune from criticism on artistic grounds, as artivism has no aesthetic component and no standard of competence. Artists naturally gravitate to providers of income, whether these are the art market, universities, private patrons, government schemes, charitable projects or public-art venues. They meet a clear demand and respond to financial incentives. My perception is that if such opportunities were removed then most artivists would leave the art field entirely.[326]

For some, income from artivism is not an issue. Assemble is a collective of architects and academics; FA is a part-time project of university tutors; Enmedio collective in Barcelona is led by a professor and comprises professionals in the visual arts. For those with salaries or wages coming from outside, artivism can be a side project which needs to do no more than cover its costs. Conversely, for artists, artivism may be their main source of income. It seems likely that, as the mechanics and funding of artivism become more commonly understood, participation in artivism will come to be considered career enhancing for non-artists (as outside interest or social activism) but career diminishing for artists (as a sign of financial failure or a stalled career), with the few exceptions of prestige artists (such as Tania Bruguera).

When we assess artivism, however much we decry parasitisation of arts funding, the elitist nature of the causes, corrupt patronage and the colonialist mindset of commissioners and practitioners, we should have compassion—even pity—for the artists who debase themselves for the most meagre of payments. Universities have produced a generation of non-artists doomed to redundancy, deliberately left unskilled, chockful of abstruse theory and puffed up with self-regard, for whom the art world (and wider society) has no use whatsoever. Where else could these graduates have gravitated to except artivist quasi-social work?

Cancel culture is our business

At the end of January 2018 (shortly after the arrival of Alistair Hudson as director), Manchester Art Gallery removed one of its most famous paintings, a Pre-Raphaelite painting. John William Waterhouse's *Hylas and the Nymphs* (1896), which depicts the Greek hero surrounded by water spirits in nude female form, was removed "to start a conversation".[327] This was done by Clare Gannaway, curator of contemporary art. She said of changes to the gallery of nudes: "there is a sense of embarrassment that we haven't dealt with it sooner." This is the common "current year" rhetorical tactic. Some act has been done (or should be done) because it is [insert current year here], which is no more than saying "we only did it now because we could get away with it". In other words, it is not a rationale but an assertion of might.

The action was supposedly temporary. "[The painting] will probably return", said Gannaway. (After protest from visitors, the painting was returned.) There was a plan to contextualise the whole museum. Contextualisation is usually done through labels and leaflets with a polemical slant. The action was a collaboration with Sonia Boyce (b. 1962), an artist and Royal Academician, best known for approaching feminist and black themes. It is troubling that a practising painter thought it appropriate to suppress work by another artist, albeit temporarily. When artivism enters the realm of retracting access to art, it flirts with censorship and toys with the power of authoritarianism. These actions may be described as playful and exploratory but the underlying aggression and egotism remain—seeds of potentially ugly and destructive tendencies that should not be cultivated.

At the end of 2020, artists acting as censors struck again. The dining room of Tate Britain is decorated by *The Expedition in Pursuit of Rare Meats* (1926-27), painted by Rex Whistler. The mural contains tiny figures of black and Chinese characters, which online race-activists/artivists considered demeaning. Their online campaign scared Tate into an ethics-committee report (one might have thought a national museum being frightened into holding an internal investigation by a social-media post was of greater ethical concern). Tate had laid itself open to such foolishness by previously conceding the legitimacy of identity politics and pandering to social-media pressure groups. Tate fudged the issue, concluding the images were "offensive" but that the mural was unremovable due to mandatory building-conservation regulations; the dining room will be decommissioned. Activists got another scalp, Tate got to shame part of its heritage and the public lost access to another art work. Temporarily sated, the activists turned their gaze to other targets.

Who stood up for the Whistler mural? Before anyone knew there was a campaign, Tate had already convened a committee— de facto acknowledgement of imminent ethical emergency—and no one had a chance to argue that Whistler may have been satirising imperialism. How many people (even supporters of the status quo) are going to risk their credibility defending art that appears either morally suspect or tonally callous? Who would risk the charge of "trivialising slavery and colonialism" in an almost certainly futile attempt to oppose righteous, self-nominated defenders of the marginalised, before a hostile or timid crowd? Who would step into that unforgiving arena with only the certain reward of execration and little chance of success? Who would take Whistler's mural as the hill upon which they would choose to die? That is how denunciation societies maintain themselves. The reward for resistance is infrequent and little; punishment can be public, swift, severe, unappealable and lasting. It can lead to shaming, ostracisation, sacking, diminishment of earning capacity, losing one's professional standing/accreditation, threats of violence or death; these can apply to the person's partner, family, friends and colleagues.

Regarding cancel culture—of which artivism is the respectable incarnation—historian Tom Holland commented that, while he was opposed to uncontrolled iconoclasm, statues commemorating those who profited from the slave trade, and were set up by those "who knew what they were doing" (i.e. later generations which "knew" that slavery was wrong), should be removed. "I would be very happy to see those come down", he commented. He drew analogies with "the English tradition of radical Protestantism".[328] He failed to clarify if he meant iconoclasm by committee or mob. The idea that artivists (with an announced distaste for historical monuments) and mobs of "anti-slavery" rioters would weigh evidence and ponder the moral culpability of subjects and commissioners of statues is absurd. In the USA, thugs defaced and toppled statues of individuals who fought for emancipation and founded charities benefiting slave descendants.[329] Holland's glib pontifications about what he was "happy to see come down" is muddle-headed social-justice piety of an intellectual with no understanding of the use his comments will be put to by agitator academics.

Artivism versus populism

Strong strains of anti-commercialism and anti-capitalism are found in artivism. That rhetoric suffuses Adam Michael's Krause's book: "Art's worth *as art* cannot be fully expressed, nor can humanity's cultural needs be met, when capitalist demands drive the production of art."[330] For the idealist, commerce is an impediment to art acting as a social device. "For art to serve its purpose—or rather, purposes—it must be radically situated within the life of a community and under the control of ordinary people. Corporate control needs to be sloughed off once and for all. Art must be decentralized and democratized."[331]

Krause's argument suggests art was commodified and thereby detached from its communal roots. Yet from the beginning of history art has been commissioned for payment. Much art would never have come into existence without commercial transactions. Also, there is nothing to prevent artists (professional or amateur) from making art available for free and giving it away. Krause draws an analogy between the commercial art world and the ecological impact of farming, claiming that mechanised farming methods put profit ahead of natural environments. This correlation between (on one hand) nature, communalism and anti-capitalism and (on the other) industry, private interests and capitalism is indicative of progressivism. The inference that what is presented as natural is also desirable shifts the onus to supporters of the status quo to justify the benefits of capitalism. It also imposes the difficulty of apparently arguing against nature and community.

"The goal should not be to simply operate *outside* the culture industry, but to supplant it."[332] So, the possibility of building parallel systems is insufficient; the aim is to destroy what exists. Krause's utopian project includes art "probing the limits of the possible and transforming minds to create a new citizenry that can wisely wield the powers of these new systems".[333] He demands "somewhat simultaneous reconstruction of art and society" to prevent resistance. This is not essentially different from the totalising authoritarianism and zealous millenarianism of the

Soviet Union or Chinese Cultural Revolution. "Art, by becoming a true avant-garde, can provide new ways of seeing, being, and understanding."[334] Krause's sentence could have been written by Mayakovsky, Breton or Debord.

Krause cites John Dewey's anti-aesthetic essay "Art as Experience" (1934) as justification for an anti-formalist approach to art. Conflating experience of life and art, Dewey erases art as a distinct category of physical material and (by extension) the possibility of drawing aesthetic distinctions between art and other material, since aesthetic separation is impossible. Once this is accepted, formalism and connoisseurship — not to mention the canon — become redundant.[335]

Krause holds up Josef Beuys as a democratiser of art. Beuys's pronouncement "Everyone is an artist" has become a rallying cry for anti-capitalists but — interestingly — not for populists. Populists tend to have conservative tastes and are not very fond of conceptualism. The reverse is reciprocated by artivists, who disdain popular artists, such as traditional favourites and "low-brow" painters such as Beryl Cook and Jack Vettriano. Populism, with its connotations of reactionary conservative masses determining their own future, is the exact antithesis of what the middle-class leftist proponents have in mind when they promote democratisation. When Paul Chan discussed one of his artivist projects, he cited Saul Alinsky (who wrote the textbook followed by socialist radicals) as an inspiration.[336] When Alinsky wrote about activists awakening social consciousness, that consciousness was congruent with the socialist outlook of organisers rather than any form of religious or racial resistance to socialism.

Those who advocate empowering people believe that they, their followers, allies and clients will seize resultant opportunities and resources.[337] If the real majority were to control culture, then the majority's values would dominate. We should not consider the elites' values to be enduring; they are fickle and cynical, as seen in reframing expressed values, regardless of truth. When the managerial elite deems immigration of benefit then "Britain has always been a mongrel nation"; when the elite supports gay rights then "Britain has always been a tolerant nation"; when the elite finds a wealth tax necessary then "the British have always had a strong sense of fairness". Imagine if artivists genuinely believed that "everyone is an artist". Should there be an emergence of widespread nativist art production that was genuinely popular, would it be welcomed or decried by artivists? Would today's artivists accept the will of the masses or would they instinctively shrink away from such sentiments? Artivism is committed to participatory cultural democracy but—like political democracy—that is curated by elite arbiters who set the parameters of acceptable outcomes. Apparent democracy provides the managerial class a defensible façade of popular decision-making while allowing the elite to make decisions.

Summary

Artivism is an important income source for artists who have difficulty producing art that appeals to consumers. Sustaining this stream of funding is vital to these artists. Academia has vested intellectual, status and financial interests in the success of artivism. Artivism includes retracting existing art and causing discomfort to certain groups. Artivism espouses democratising art but intends resources to be allocated to favoured groups. Artivists are not hypocritical because their principles are held tactically; in-group signalling and preference, as well as supremacy in resource control, are the only enduring principles.

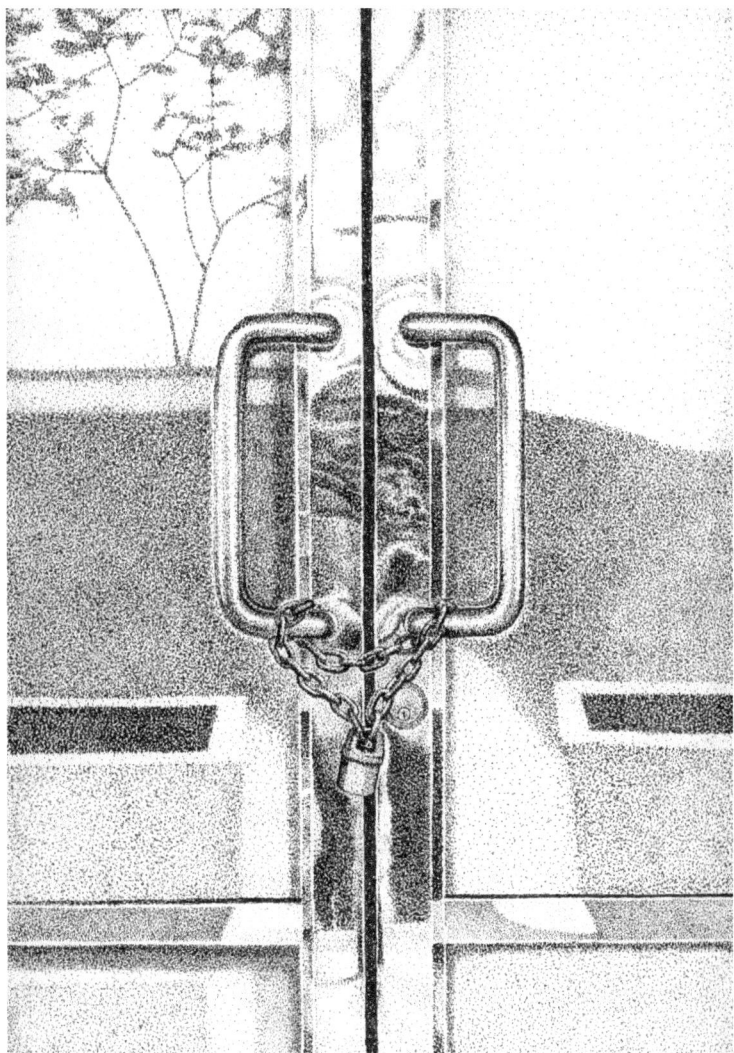

Case Study

Artivism for Migration

Cuban performance artist Tania Bruguera (b. 1968) is credited as a founder of artivism due to her conception of useful art (*arte útil*). Bruguera highlights "the enduring social and political reality of the Cuban experience in which the utopian dream has been shattered by the hard facts of daily life".[338] Apparent in Bruguera's activity is a clear conflict between her socialist beliefs and the repressive reality of Cuba's socialist regime. Her actions include performances by the artist, volunteers and members of the public, as well as documentation and installations. In 2010, she initiated *Immigrant Movement International*, a five-year project to improve the lot of immigrants in New York City. Migration advocacy is a key part of Bruguera's activities and is a common cause for artivist action worldwide. "Since relocating to the United States in 1997 the artist has become a world citizen, living and working in such cities as Chicago, Paris, Havana, and New York, and traveling regularly and extensively to create her art and to teach."[339]

In October 2021, the Cuban government bribed Bruguera to leave the island, leaving behind her Hannah Arendt artivist foundation based in Havana. Bruguera had called for people to boycott the Havana Biennal, a significant cultural event and generator of hard cash from international visitors. Under pressure to depart, Bruguera negotiated with the authorities the release of

25 political prisoners in return for leaving the island. Once the prisoners were released, Bruguera was escorted by security personnel to the airport to ensure she carried out her promise to depart. She went to the USA to join Harvard University as a lecturer. It is difficult not to interpret this episode as a socially conservative government identifying subversion of an artivist promoter of globalist values and removing her from the country.[340]

Romanian artivist Carmen Manuela Popa (slogan: "World for humanity") runs Migrant Integration Lab, "A global device for sustainable integration designed by B1-AKT Leading Sustainable Strategies & Paragon Communication." The mission is described as follows:

> Integration is a concept that has become a buzzword, and its meaning is interpreted in many different ways. We understand integration as a dynamic process involving two or more parties that work together to make a cohesive, balanced and harmonious whole. At Migrant Integration Lab we are contributing to making human communities successful and sustainable while organically embracing diversity. Our Labs are based on transnational frameworks that are giving policy-makers a new lens with which to develop innovative public programs, and public–private partnerships across borders. And because of the economic implications of transnationalism, it provides opportunities for businesses, social entrepreneurs, and governments.[341]

B1-AKT "offers you the most innovative, leading and sustainable solutions in complex project steering, international management, intercultural training, holistic communication. We do it via strategic advisory services, leading training services and innovation labs".[342] This Paris-based organisation had 12 members of staff in 2021 and had associated partners worldwide. It lists its funders as multinational corporations, universities and departments of the French national and regional governments; partners include migration and refugee organisations.³⁴³ One partner is Humans for Women, an intersectional feminist association.³⁴⁴

UN Women promotes gender equality, seeking to establish a single standard worldwide, regardless of local culture and values of elected governments. One route is through artivism:

> As part of the Generation Equality campaign, seven distinguished local artists—from Albania, Georgia, Kosovo, Moldova, North Macedonia, Turkey, and the curator of the initiative from the United States of America—are starting a conversation on gender equality through mural art in Europe and Central Asia. A mural is a painting on the wall in a public space that has the unique power to reach broad audiences and engage citizens in dialogue on social issues that are vital to the city or community. From ancient times until now, vibrant murals promote new urban narratives and social change through art.³⁴⁵

One doubts that a conversation that included the local population saying "We prefer to keep our gender roles traditional" would be one that UN Women would find acceptable. However we feel individually about the subject, it seems unarguable that supranational bodies seek to impose universal standards in a manner reminiscent of colonialism, regardless of the wishes of local populations.

The Atlantic Council (an American internationalist think-tank) featured on its website an article about Artlords. Artlords was a group of Afghan street artists who created murals in Kabul depicting a woman who had been lynched, distinctive vehicles driven by warlords and other paintings criticising failings of Afghan society.³⁴⁶ They painted a mural featuring George Floyd, using his case as an example of racism.³⁴⁷ International organisations tend to support artivism in non-Western countries when it supports international values. Such artivism reinforces Western values and suggests popular support for those values among the populace, something that is not necessarily true. The fragility of artivism seems to be borne out by the rapid collapse of the 2001–

2021 Western-backed democracy in Afghanistan. As soon as the Afghan government fled Kabul, Taliban members painted over all murals depicting people.

These are a handful of the thousands of pro-migration artivist activities that are promoted through state and quasi-state channels. Utile art is an expression of elite values in that it goes further than most of the population or political parties are willing to support, taking a fringe position, albeit a "radically compassionate extreme". Rather than making socially conscious art that encourages charity, social reform or legislation, as happened in the past,[348] today's utile artist takes it upon herself to intervene and undertake social action that has no electoral or popular mandate. Often, a visiting foreign artivist is in direct conflict with the wishes of the indigenous population, which research shows is consistently resistant to mass immigration.[349] Bruguera — "a world citizen" — is typical of the globalist elite, which agitates for mass movement of people without taking responsibility (much less living with) the deleterious impact of migration. There are advantages to immigration but even raising the statistically measurable negative consequences of immigration is dismissed as xenophobia by the upper levels of society.

We could class migration advocacy by global artivists as a form of colonialism — increasing resources and influence of a newly arrived community at the expense of the resident majority population. If a utile artist were to advocate for preservation of an indigenous population in (say) a British locality — as a form of anti-colonial action — such measures would meet with disapproval from the art establishment. This tendency to see high migration and mixed ethnicities as both not only desirable but a normative state, I have previously described as "national cosmopolitanism".[350] National cosmopolitanism leads its followers to distort and rewrite history out of both a desire to be more inclusive (and enact retrospective vengeance) but also an inability to accept the difference between their view of history and its obdurate reality.

Whatever one's attitude is towards these social issues, it is undeniable that the art establishment's biases are declared through revealed preferences by supporting certain artivist projects and rejecting others. Artivists perform the same role of student radicals on university campuses. Inspired by staff, they advance radical ideas, take direct action, push the envelope for acceptable behaviour and claim new territory. At the same time, the establishment is technically not responsible for the actions and can disclaim them as "starting a conversation", whilst privately condoning the actions and advancing its agenda. Once an event has occurred, it can be cited as precedent. Objection to a future event can be defeated thus: "Event X took place before this proposed activity, so it is just following accepted practice." The progressivist ratchet moves in one direction alone: leftward. Movements leftwards (framed as "reforms" or "innovations" rather than encroachments or impositions) are minor temporary explorations, supposedly provisional, but they become semi-permanent entitlements or precedents. If one objects that an innovation is contrary to the public good or breaches legal parameters, that objection will be treated as a first step towards retraction of all minority rights and a signal of a reactionary wave that will sweep away all protections and tolerance. Language framing acts as social conditioning, making the ratchet movement seem like inevitable progress rather than a managerial elite forcefully undermining right-elite tradition, in ways that are rarely subject to popular vote or informed debate.

The globally-oriented art elite is neither politically uniform nor coordinated but there is little establishment support in the West—in the realm of contemporary art—for art that is nationalist, nativist, socially or aesthetically conservative or anti-globalist in outlook. Indeed, when the United Nations produced a report on the creative economies of the developing world, it identified these economies as a key route to making countries conform to international standards ("policy coherence"). The UN and allied bodies see cultural conformity through government policy as a plank of globalisation.[351] Where one does encounter art embodying conservative values, it is produced by non-Western artists and immigrant-descended creators in the West, and is often presented as an act of reclamation or resistance by immigrants towards Western values. The conclusion that seems indicated is that *a priori* attitudes among the art elite are that the West, white-majority nations, Christianity, capitalism and commodification of art are undesirable and their "opposites" are desirable. All theory and strategy in the field of state-supported art is adapted to accommodate these precepts.

During this research, I encountered no project which opposed mass migration. This suggests that only certain social attitudes towards nationality and social cohesion are considered permissible by gatekeeping authorities.

Six

The Psychology of Artivism

So far, we have looked at the mechanics of artivism. We should touch upon the psychology and politics that drive artivists. In Chapter 2 we briefly looked at the paternalistic colonialism of artivists when acting as spokesmen for others. Here are additional factors.

Solutions or trade-offs?

Artivism-as-social-action often springs from a leftist social-constructivist outlook. The leftist sees suboptimal situations such as poverty, inequality, homelessness and racial/sexual discrimination (let alone gentrification, lack of representation within the arts and access to culture) as unarguably unfair and indisputably problematic. Assumptions about injustice and necessity of remedy are automatically made. These issues are thought of as problems that have particular causes and for which solutions can (given sufficient knowledge, money, collective will, action and legislation) be undertaken. As Burnham puts it:

> The guilt of the liberal causes him to feel obligated to try to *do something* about any and every social problem, to cure every social evil. This feeling, too, is non-rational: the liberal must try to cure the evil even if he has no knowledge of the suitable medicine or, for that matter, of the nature of the disease; he must *do something* about the social problem even when there is

no objective reason to believe that what he does can solve the problem—when, in fact, it may well aggravate the problem instead of solving it.[352]

The idea that some (probably all) of these situations are irresolvable does not occur to proponents of artivism. The leftist—unlike the conservative—fails to conceive of complex situations arising in a world where there are no solutions, only trade-offs. The conservative sees human flaws as the cause of suboptimal situations, that might be improved but never resolved; the leftist sees structural flaws as the cause of suboptimal situations that can be perfected, given time, knowledge and power.[353]

The effectiveness of artivism is secondary to the self-satisfaction and in-group signalling the action affords. A given response to a situation is practically arbitrary, driven by values. Take the subject of immigration. The elite value in the West is that immigration is overwhelmingly positive and should be encouraged and normalised. Are we to believe that every artist who supports migration could not (with suitable institutional and financial support) make artivism putting the contrary case? It seems a matter of political conditioning utilising incentives of social approval, professional prestige and monetary reward. The vast majority of ostensibly politically committed artists follow the lead given them. In other words, few people have deeply considered ethical positions and fewer still are those who are willing to suffer for these.

Boundaries: protection or prohibition?

Boundaries to leftists are barriers, impediments, devices for separating people who would be naturally harmonious and cooperative. For the conservative, boundaries are ways of demarcating groups, understanding the world, providing privacy, placing limits on an individual's or community's responsibility (and power); defining material helps in discussions and makes the world comprehensible. Conservatives defend borders but leftists always seek to remove them. Transdisciplinary practices are beloved of academics on the left because they seem to open up exciting cross-currents of inquiry. These undermine restricted fields and undermine sites of fixed authority. When it comes to artivism, the leftist enjoys transgressing boundaries of art, politics, social action and everyday life. He likes unsettling the viewer's assumptions, seeking to undermine preconceptions. The rationale is that once someone is detached from received prejudices, he will respond in a more open manner.

G.K. Chesterton devised an analogy of a walker who encounters a fence in a field. Not perceiving the reason for the fence, the walker considers it an atavistic obstruction and removes it. Chesterton argued that, just like this fence, traditions perform useful functions that are not immediately apparent. He wrote that no man should dismantle a tradition without fully understanding its origins and use. The progressive is automatically inclined to remove every fence (trusting in the abilities of his generation to overcome any negative effects); the conservative is automatically inclined to retain every fence (trusting in wisdom refined over generations to be superior to the abilities of his generation). Artivist interdisciplinary action is instinctive fence removal.

Artivism and anti-humanism

In one sense, progressivist materialism is a form of humanism. That is, it accepts nothing transcendental or eternal, and does not recognise objective morality. In another respect, it displays troubling misanthropy and anti-humanism. At the root of much eco-activism is a mistrust of humans and this finds its plainest appearance in modern population-control principles, which began with Malthus in 1798. The desire to manage mankind to a degree where populations are deemed expendable finds its way into scientific racism and eugenics. It may seem peculiar to mention this in relation to progressivism, with its ostensible ethos of compassion and utilitarianism, but the magnanimity of scientific socialism, globalism and atheism turns so often into brutalisation of people. Reforming and controlling untidy, unruly humanity into a scientifically organised system is as much the goal of the utilitarian progressive as much as that of the radical fascist or authoritarian socialist.

Can we detect anti-humanist tendencies in the art field? Firstly, commitment to collectivism by groups including Marxists, feminists and race separatists displays disdain for dissent, doubt and pleasure. A chilling certainty enters their pronouncements. When facing criticism of women artists, Maura Reilly wrote, "Provocations like those [...] should not tolerated", and "Should *The Independent* be printing such overtly sexist statements?"[354] Likewise, "the myth of solitariness [...] the reality of community" could be a reminder of sisterly unity or a sneer against the lone dissenter.[355] Art collectives and artivists, especially when they have a commitment to Marxism, dismiss our innate tendency to admire accomplishments of unique artists. "[...T]he prevailing cult of the individual artist is problematic for those whose goal is to work with others, generally in collaborative projects with democratic ideals. Many artists look for ways to renounce not only object-making but authorship altogether [...]"[356] One member of an art collective took up his work to "reject a culture of hyper-individualism".[357]

Secondly, we find casual radicalism expressed among the company of comrades. Speaking of the American riots of 2020, artivist Hannah Black thought that action should precede analysis, negotiation or demands. She said: "I think you need to burn things down then talk about it." She spoke of collective action and losing oneself within violence: "You don't know yet what your individual contribution might be in the next intense revolutionary moment."[358] The offhand support for violence, arson and art destruction by people gathered in group action indicates a thuggish disdain for others. Futurism lauded violence, as did Breton.

Thirdly, the rise of left-wing identity politics has seen the compartmentalisation of people according to race granted respectability. Twenty years ago, such talk would have been deemed stereotyping and racism of the rankest kind. As usual with scientific racism, there is a grim dehumanising quality.

Consider this statement from B.O.S.S.: "[...] Black, brown, working class, disabled, queer bodies are desirable, quickly dispensable, but never sustainably cared for."[359] Another artivist wrote of her motivation to make films: "[...] mainstream British media of the 1980s did not image brown female bodies [...]"[360] United We Dream artivists write, "In the past couple of months we have seen immigrant communities, people of color, Black communities suffer injustices. However, this is not the first time Black and brown bodies have suffered injustices."[361] Commonly, people are reduced to "voices". This language (which emanated from race and gender courses in universities) has swept across the art world and betrays an earnest racial essentialism that appeals to those people who have a low tolerance threshold for ambiguity and impaired empathy.

These terms are frequently found in progressive circles. They are used in a direct manner too often to be paraphrasing or summarising attitudes of an uncaring capitalist society. Such dehumanising talk of people as "bodies" and "voices" reminds us of sociopaths who join mass movements to improve the lot of humanity but undertake torture and execution. How telling that groups founded for social action (dedicated to the welfare of people) avoid the words "people" and "persons" because they imply varied experiences, life choices, affinities, passions and capacities. This demonstrates a drive to anonymise, collectivise and treat people as little more than utile drones. If this vision seems bleak, it should be. It is the vision of utopians who openly meditate on the potential of trans-humanism, post-humanism and universal systems. These attitudes are shared by people who lead governments, supra-national bodies, charities, NGOs and organisations with the power and money to implement their ideas. It is these archetypes who governed scientific states which engaged in eugenics, mass deportation, political correction, war and genocide. We should always be on our guard against crusading anti-humanism of social utopians no matter how banal an opening gambit may seem.

Before leaving this topic, it is worth mentioning the attraction of artivism for those subject to the well-studied self-victimisation complex and the Dark Triad (narcissism, Machiavellianism and psychopathy). That is in addition to those exploiting the intersectional oppression stack, where those deemed most oppressed can claim the highest privileges. Artivism is an ideal channel for those who wish to exploit or control others, because it supplies good-faith colleagues and audiences, plentiful resources and high-status rewards for participants. By no means are all artivists exploiters, but artivism provides myriad opportunities to manipulators compelled by their psychological make-up.

Warning should be taken from how rarely artivists mention delight and pleasure and how often their statements are riven with anger, resentment and malice. This alone should tip us off to be wary of rewarding such individuals. The opportunity to vilify and humiliate others under the guise of defending minorities and seeking justice gives permission for ordinary people to indulge their basest drives without consequence.

Summary

Artivism attracts utopians, materialists and individuals predisposed to a social-constructivist outlook who yearn for purpose; the constituency of those attracted to artivism is determined by temperament. Artivism generates self-worth and allows artists to form communities and do (apparent) social good. Artivism provides a home to Machiavellian manipulators and those driven by righteous anger. General acceptance as to the worth of causes supported by artivism means that artivists are rarely challenged or forced to explain actions to a critical audience. Artivism — being a wide practice rather than a coherent organised movement — does not limit itself or discipline its own.

Case Study

North African Artivism

The Arab Spring uprisings in 2010–12 were a revolt against the ruling elite across North Africa and the Near East. Egyptian Streets is an English-language website/mobile phone application, established in 2012. "Egyptian Streets is an independent, young, and grass roots news media organization aimed at providing readers with an alternate depiction of events that occur on Egyptian and Middle Eastern streets, and to establish an engaging social platform for readers to discover and discuss the various issues that impact the region."[362] Topics that the website articles, podcasts and videos cover include sex education, gender stereotypes, alternative therapy, street culture, crime and news stories.

> Egyptian Streets has also collaborated with numerous non-governmental organizations and activist groups to promote a variety of social issues, including poverty, women's issues, racism, environmental issues, animal rights, education and more. These collaborations, which have often included the featuring of these organizations' causes, are aimed at driving social change through the promotion of grass-roots movements. Among the groups which Egyptian Streets has supported or collaborated with are Earth Hour, Dignity Without Borders, Heya, the Goethe Institut, the World Food Programme, Animal Care in Egypt, Creative Industry 2014, Sinai Reef and more.[363]

There has been analysis of artivism (principally popular music, street art, dance, cartoons) in anti-government action in Tunis, which led to the downfall of the Tunisian government in 2011.[364] The use of social media as a device for gathering "flash mobs", for purposes of protesting or agitating, has been described as a crossover between performance art and political assembly.[365] The artivists there were clear that their aim was either the removal of the government or reform so thorough that it would effectively amount to appointment of a new government. Analysis was conducted by a staff member of Turning Tables, an international artivist NGO based in Denmark, which had a presence in Tunisia until 2014.[366] A noteworthy distinction is that Arab Spring artivism (contrasting with that in the West) was not supported by governments. The degree of popular support for the artivism is unclear, but the opposition of the Tunisian establishment towards artivism was clear. Protestors, activists and artivists were arrested and gaoled for anti-government action. In the early 2000s, the Egyptian government had cracked down on Heavy Metal listeners, arresting 100 fans in a single purge, describing them as devil-worshippers, drug-takers and promiscuous subversives.[367] Whether or not they had been subversives previously, government-persecuted metalheads would become leading activists in the Arab Spring.[368]

> [During the Arab Spring protests] cultural producers, intellectuals and politicians are ask[ed] foundational questions about the role of government in the field of culture and vice versa. But whereas Western artists and institutions have often benefited from cultural state subsidies, assuring that arts and culture are not controlled solely by the market powers, worries in other regions is that it in fact gives Cultural Ministries the power to pick and choose according to their own agenda. As Pahwa & Winegar[369] claim: "Others counter that the state has an interest in supporting art that fits a political agenda or that state employees direct funds to their own art and that of friends and relatives."[370]

So, artivism can work against the establishment. Artivism in Tunisia in 2011 was encouraged by supporters of European-style secularism and economic reform and by supporters of Islamism, both groups excluded from government and positions of official power. This is a classic example of a revolution being led and organised not by the majority of the population but by excluded power elites which influenced action and narrative (through mass media, social media, visible protest, etc.). The intelligentsia and creatives were the vanguard. Whether or not the revolution in question was supported by the majority of the population is moot. The point is about the leadership and direction.

The 20 February 2011 Movement (20FM) in Morocco was in a similar situation. 20FM protestors issued this declaration: "We don't believe in censorship and Moroccan filmmaking laws. Cameras are our weapons. We believe that the Centre Cinematographique Marocain is a corporatist institution designed, under tyranny, to control Moroccan films and contain or censor any critique against the Makhzen [Moroccan state]. In the spirit of peaceful disobedience, we shoot films and encourage others to shoot films without authorisation as a form of protest."[371] 20FM's platform was similar to the Tunisian opposition's, namely more democratic participation, less corruption, more political freedom and economic reforms. The European Institute for the Mediterranean reported on the Moroccan situation. It is a think-tank based in Barcelona, receiving corporate and governmental funding. The institute concluded its report on 20FM thus:

> [...] the European Union, the United States and other Moroccan partners need to undertake a thorough assessment of the feasibility of their objectives in the field of democracy promotion *vis-à-vis* the country. Their programmes do not seem to take into account the changing nature of youth activism in the post-2011 era in Morocco. While they are still supporting service-provider associations, which offer no contribution to the democratisation process, the programmes dedicated to supporting politically-motivated forms of youth activism fall short of expectations.[372]

In other words, international organisations and foreign governments could support artivism as a means of political change. As these movements seek to replace governments, we can infer that artivism is seen as a legitimate route to regime change.

Revolutions and uprisings in non-Western countries are often supported by Western intelligence services. States such as (say) the USA find a way of backing and co-opting almost any foreign rebel faction or governing regime, regardless of politics, unless the ideology of that group is explicitly religious or isolationist. The extensive documented history of overt and covert backing for rebels in non-Western states could be framed like so: rebels are adopted by the power elite of the West. Washington DC-based International Center for Nonviolent Conflict supports and encourages anti-government action (including artivism) worldwide. Ahmed Bensaada claims that the leaders of the Arab Spring were inspired, recruited, trained and paid by US governmental organisations.[373] Other US federally-supported NGOs include the National Democratic Institute for International Affairs, International Republican Institute (IRI), Free Trade Union Institute, Center for International Private Enterprise, Middle East Partnership Initiative, Aspen Institute and Freedom House (FH) — all of which act to further US international interests in foreign states in the guise of "democracy promotion".

The Academy of Change (formed of Egyptian dissidents) and the Egyptian Muslim Brotherhood both took up *From Dictatorship to Democracy* (1993), a handbook on non-violent revolutionary action by Gene Sharp. They published partial translations and adapted the writings prior to the Egyptian revolution of 2011. They did not credit the American author. "[… T]hese groups knew that they might soon be cast as foreign inspired traitors and puppets of US imperialism."[374] FH and IRI both trained anti-government activists ahead of the 2011 elections.[375] The Centre for Applied Nonviolent Action and Strategies in Belgrade acted as a training and coordination base.[376] Clearly, both the US government and Western NGOs contributed to the overthrow of regimes during the Arab Spring.

Tunisian and Moroccan artivism could be seen as backed by the establishment—the Western establishment—indirectly through organisations such as Turning Tables and others. Not that any of these NGOs is necessarily controlled, influenced or funded by any government, but that Western NGOs generally share values (democracy, secularism, progressive social policies, internationalism) which are aligned with the interests of the dominant elite in Western states.[377] Artivism on behalf of the establishment elite is a means of using supposedly independent voices to reframe elite values, bypassing political consent, enacting acceleration of the erosion of traditions and demoralising the majority population by asserting elite values not majority values. Artivism by rival power elites favours dissident values and personnel in much the same way—minus erosion of traditional values, if this elite is rightist. Independent spontaneous artivism does exist, but mainly small-scale and at a community level, unrecognised by museums, publishers and mass media.

It is important to assess links without being too influenced by sympathies regarding individual situations. It is entirely reasonable to support animal welfare, women's education and mental-health provision whilst also being clear-eyed about advantages that the overall agendas of artivist movements and platforms offer to international bodies. Consider that eroding one area of a national culture (even an odious one) advances erosion in other areas, thereby diminishing the autonomy of that nation. Progressivism never stops; it is incremental and endless. When a solution to an apparent problem accords with a supposed global standard, it functions as part of the process of globalisation, whether or not it was intended that way. Localism is the best defence against global values, laws and control; localism entails areas of advantage (local culture, strong communities, preservation of language) and disadvantage (fewer rights for women, discrimination, lower standards of health). This is a difficult issue. Remedying suffering can advance the interests of internationalism, which seeks to erase autonomy and tradition to the overall detriment to the population. I offer this observation without being able to offer a solution.

Seven

Resisting Artivism

This chapter will outline strategies of resistance for individuals, groups, organisations and states that could prevent artivism consuming an ever-greater share of art resources. This assumes there is any willingness of elites to give up state channels for promotion (through artivism) of their values.

Detaching artivism from the elite

This book sets out how complicated are the dynamics of the conjunction of art and politics. Artivism is no grassroots movement of individuals forming a community to fight against power; it is not a psy-op or controlled opposition directed by authorities. It can be both at the same time, blended and altering over time. It can also be simply an individual finding a creative outlet or chance to make money. Most artivism encountered via social media, viewed in newspapers or experienced at a festival was endorsed by elites. The original creator may be a renegade and anti-establishment type but these ideas reach a wide audience because people with money and influence find the cause worthy or useful. Creators, participants, venue staff and audience may all act in good faith and be completely immersed in the experience but it is supporting charities, sponsors and civil servants who decide which projects are backed.

From a sceptical position, is it not best to be critical of elites? We could try to hold them responsible, if for no other reason than to curb their excesses. Rather than nudge policies and propaganda through artivism, would it not be better to have policies made transparent and arguments set out forthrightly? Rather than governance by experts and influencers, how about governance by representatives elected by the population? This is idealistic but aspirational. Drawing some line between what is acceptable for public arts funding and what is unacceptable is a worthwhile endeavour, no matter how difficult.

This book rests on a number of precepts. (1) Public funding of arts has benefits for the population. (2) All funding of art necessarily has political consequences for funders, producers and consumers. (3) Art is not pure and is influenced to some degree by conditions of production and reception. (4) The state acting as the prime arbiter of taste and content of art has potentially dangerous implications. (5) The state is delimited and operates through central government, local government, NGOs, universities, partner companies and charities; complementarily, these bodies also work through the state and through each other. (6) These bodies and the state exert influence on art and through art. (7) It is to the benefit of producers and consumers to detach art from the influence of funders; it is not to the benefit of funders to do this; funders will seek to evade restrictions. Artivism is an outgrowth of social activism which has been given the status of art by those who wish to gain resources. It is amplified by the managerial elite due to its utility. The support is reciprocal but not equal, in that artivists benefit greatly from elite support with the elite benefiting in low-level manner. This matches Abbing's analysis of why the state finances art.[378]

During the examination of hundreds of documents (books, theses, essays, statements, interviews and websites), I never encountered a single artivist or artivism advocate who acknowledged that there are ethical issues regarding artivist use of resources reserved for fine art. To committed supporters of activism, there are no valid grounds for questioning the ethics of artivism or restricting artivism.

One effective way of undermining artivist claims in the public sphere is to present to those in positions of influence the argument that artivism is a territory grab of resources earmarked for art without any consideration for the wishes of public, donors or the foundational principles of arts organisations. Artivism goes against what most people consider to be legitimate art, but if artivism does not infringe the rights of others, most people would not object to private funds supporting such activities. Make it clear to decision-makers that if a project is worthwhile or popular, charity or corporate funding can replace public funds.

Potential routes for reducing artivism

Here are summary suggestions of measures to reduce widespread state encouragement of activism-as-art. This excludes political fine art that is recognisably fine art in form and material.

1. Ethics

Explain that it is unethical to allow activists to appropriate public resources reserved for the arts. This action excludes competent artists from opportunities that are rightfully theirs and it deprives the general public of the art that they would otherwise encounter due to public-art provision.

2. Exclusion

Artivism should not be permitted within publicly-funded museums, art venues or festivals. Even if the artivism proposed is cost-free to the public, it uses public facilities and receives state/regional imprimatur of official approval in order to advance its agenda. Allowing privately-funded artivism in public venues merely provides administrators with a work-around, so this should also be banned.

3. Defunding

No arts body, venue, group or individual which engages in artivism should receive public money because artivism is political campaigning. Even if funds were provided for other reasons (i.e. a general grant made to an artist who also engages in artivism), this would amount to cross-subsidisation; it should therefore be banned from receiving public money.

4. Reduction

If the state were to reduce funding for arts then there would be less poor-quality art made to meet state quotas. There would be greater incentive for artists to appeal to patrons, investors and the public, thereby raising overall production quality. This would encourage marginally-economically productive creators to leave the industry, improving opportunities and incomes for artists dedicated to making art-as-art. Artivism is a symptom of a wider malaise of state interference in cultural production. If the state's art budget were reduced, state influence would contract, allowing arts production to potentially flourish in less politically directed ways.

5. Education

No state-funded school, college or university should receive funding for courses, programmes or modules dedicated to—or featuring—artivism. This should extend to extra-curricular activity supported by any publicly funded educational establishment. State bodies should be able to lower or withdraw funding to educational establishments that breach this rule. If student-artists wish to practise artivism in their private time or otherwise outside of work submitted for assessment, that is their choice.

6. Enforcement

Enforce existing regulations regarding conduct in public and charity sectors. When arts charities break regulations, retract their status, require repayment of public money, reprimand or fire venue administrators who misspend money or use their positions as political platforms. Harming the reputation of a public establishment is no different from damaging public property. Arts administrators must abide by an employment code that treats their role as a custodian of an organisation. Said staff must act relatively fairly and impartially; they must not bar artists on the basis of the artist's political outlook (actual or presumed).

This definition cannot include all artivism. We should expect some artivism to accrue at the edges. This is not a problem, as artivism *per se* is not a problem. It is an activity that depends on (a) money, (b) institutional support, (c) elite-class support, (d) peer support and (e) critical/theoretical justification. If points (a) and (b) are reduced, then the artivism that the state itself generates will be reduced.

If anything can be art (according to postmodernism) and if art must be useful (according to utilitarianism), then the ideal vehicle is artivism. Like a predatory pike released into a carp pool, artivism will remorselessly consume all. By its very nature, artivism will occupy all resources reserved for art. As with all invasive species, it is much better to prevent a species being introduced than to eradicate it once it is loose. Any who wish to save the public-arts funding model must reject artivism wholesale before it destabilises the ecosystem of public arts, whether or not such action exposes the objector to the risk of shaming or isolation.

The goal of these recommendations is not to end artivism; the goal is to reduce artivism in public arts and public education to only infrequent and marginal cases. If this is not done, artivism will suffocate the public fine arts that generations have cherished and perpetuated. If artivism flourishes through private, commercial or community channels, then it serves a function. If it fails to find fertile ground, then it is proven to be artificially stimulated and it deserves whatever fate awaits it.

Conclusions

A general consumer of culture may ask, "What threat is there in involving children in an art project about ecosystems or a scheme informing immigrant women about their legal rights? Surely this book, full of the worst examples of excess and unpleasantness found in artivism, is another attempt to manufacture a moral panic…"

As far as those two notional projects go, there is nothing wrong with them *per se*. If these projects were not funded as public art and were the limit of artivism, there would be no concern. The difficulty comes when they claim public resources as fine art. Now the precedent is set, public arts—formerly measured by standards of competence and merit—are open to artivists who are far less benign than the organisers of those projects. Artivism encourages zealotry, aggression, iconoclasm and assaults on common standards. The foundations of public arts have been so thoroughly compromised that basic principles have already been overturned. None of the examples cited in this book are exaggerated. I excluded the most egregious of stunts, including induced vomiting, public orgies, burning animals alive[379] and an activist nailing his scrotum to a cathedral door. Listing these instances of puerility and appealing to readers' sense of decency would hardly have made a fair hearing for artivism.

Artists should speak freely. That does not mean they should have automatic access to public resources for political action which has little or no artistic worth.[380] Plentiful private, corporate, charity and community funding is available for political action dressed as art; supply of non-state money for art has never been higher. There is no contradiction in supporting free speech and suggesting states retract funding for such speech. This is because state sanction (by providing platforms and funding) encourages types of speech that would otherwise have little appeal. It creates a false market, allowing niche activity (little different from propaganda) to thrive without detectable support. ("[… T]he relative indifference of the putative audience for publicly funded works", as one writer gently puts it.)[381] Not only this, but material can be aggressive and intended to perpetuate grudges between groups. Through its sponsorship, the state is making a poison that would otherwise not exist; the state then administers this poison to the population, calling it medicine.

Political art is only as good or bad as its art and politics and the artist's ability to cogently synthesise them. Action-as-art is another matter. Regardless of the merit of causes, we can posit that continuing to platform such divisive material—especially when it reflects only the establishment-approved section of political viewpoints, rather than a full spectrum—is an unsustainable model. Is it fair that tax money is used to berate a whole society for mild social attitudes and impute to historical (retrospectively judged) "crimes" on the basis of parentage?

Beyond the unfairness of such actions, state art reveals something so unsettling that most of us turn away our faces at the implications. Doesn't such a system of tax-funded alienation of the population seem a power play? Does it not demonstrate underlying contempt? The troubling conclusion is that the managerial technocratic elite's degradation of the populace—its history, arts and common values—is deliberate. Consider the joyful malice and vicious anger of artivism—its sweeping assumptions of privilege and discrimination—and ask yourself, is this healthy for makers and consumers of artivism? Consider regimes that placed at the apex of their culture material motivated by hate. Are those societies ones that we wish to emulate?

Readers are invited to make their own assessments about the motivation for, and value of, individual acts of artivism described in this book. Artivism is capable of being relatively apolitical; in practice, artivism supported by the state does not oppose progressivism. Most artivism—certainly all that you can find in the public arts—champions the minority and sets up the majority as agents of oppression. It is hard to see prominent artivism as anything other than a battering ram of the technocratic elite used upon both established values of conservatism and the anti-elitist reactionary population, largely working class. Recall Burnham's warning: "The rule of the élite is based upon force and fraud."[382]

If rules regarding charitable status, impartiality of publicly-funded bodies, ringfencing art funding and controlling activist staff are not enforced, then public trust will diminish rapidly. If antagonising audiences continues, then patience will be strained to breaking point. If the model that seemed to serve most of us so well is to remain, then the excesses, elitism and corruption rampant in the British public arts must be effectively and promptly curtailed.

But maybe it would be better to lose trust in that system. Perhaps the poison was not introduced to the system but was always present within it. Consider state artivism's authoritarianism, impatience, globalism, neophilia, progressivism, selective framing of truth and exploitation of client groups. Do these seem like accretions of incidental attitudes or do they indicate core values of the technocrats who established the system? Consider also the way that every institution established (or substantially reshaped) according to Enlightenment liberalism has fallen to progressive subversion. Does that not seem indicative of an inherent foundational flaw?

A consequent conclusion is that state-sponsored art in modern times was always action to demoralise and humiliate the managerial elite's opponents—the general population. Emergence of artivism was not primarily due to entropy or opportunism but an inevitable end stage. It could be that pushing the limits of what was acceptable was always the purpose of exploratory vanguardism, measuring how far the managerial elite could debase foundational beliefs that held them in check. Perhaps the golden era of public arts in the UK (roughly 1945–2000) was always a precursor to the elite taking off the gloves and using funding in ways that went beyond preference for stylistic avant-gardism and moved on to active promotion of globalism, with palpable contempt for the general population. It was a show of unchallenged supremacy, all the while mocking the deepest beliefs of people who had to pay for it. The patronage of minorities-as-minorities was always the final stage. Two interpretations of this latest stage are (a) inadvertent revelation of the ruling class's values and (b) explicit instatement of minorities as client groups of the ruling class. Both could, according to elite theory, be viable explanations. In the technocratic usurpation of established norms of the West—artistic, political, economic, cultural, religious, familial, sexual, demographic—state-funded avant-gardism was a masterful elite action.

Even now, I am personally undecided about whether or not either of these final conclusions is a reflection of the truth.

Appendices

A: Correspondence between the author and ICA, 2018

2 October 2018

Dear Mr Kalmar

On Monday, 1 October 2018 the ICA held an event entitled "The Annual Friends of the Institute of Contemporary Arts Dinner in Honour of Chelsea Manning" (the "Event"). The guest, Chelsea Manning, is described in the ICA press release (14 August 2018) (the "Press Release") as an "American activist". That Press Release continues:

> This invite-only event will be preceded by a public Q&A hosted by the ICA at the Royal Institution, in which Chelsea Manning will address the rise of artificial intelligence; the state of the data economy and the role of algorithms and AI in public policy; the role of digital technologies in creating more transparency and democracy, from Panama Papers to Snowden, but also undermining democracy, like Cambridge Analytica; and her role in supporting J20 defendants and as advocate for LGBTQ+ rights. This is the second Friends' Dinner, established in 2017 by the ICA's new Director Stefan Kalmár to pay tribute to a global public figure aligning with the historic mission as well as the current work of the Institute.

The Press Release nowhere discusses the artistic function of the Event. The guest is a political and social activist who is not an artist, has not produced creative work and has no displayed expertise in the arts. The discussion was not billed as a discussion about art. The conclusion one draws is that the Event was expressly political. Indeed, the Press Release describes Manning as "a global figure aligning with the historic mission as well as the current work of the Institute", which draws an explicit link between the guest's social-political activism and the ICA's activity.

You are quoted as stating in *Frieze* magazine website (14 August 2018) the following:

> Can the ICA be an organization that revitalizes the belief of civic responsibility in cultural institutions, but also of progress within society? I think that we have the right conditions to make a strong case for that.[383]

This statement and the Press Release suggest the Event was intended as a celebration of the guest's activism and supported social/political-campaigning activity by the ICA itself. It is reasonable to conclude that the Event was political activity. As such it raises three issues that need publicly addressing:

1. Contravention of the ICA Memorandum of Association

The ICA Memorandum of Association of 22 July 1947, subsequently updated, (the "Memorandum") specifies the purposes and activities of the ICA. The Event falls outside those purposes and activities as defined in the Memorandum, most specifically Article 3(i), which describes the area of activity of the ICA as the visual arts.[384] The Event was—as expressly stated in the Memorandum—an occasion to honour a political activist with no known connection to the visual arts. Thus the Event seems to contravene the Memorandum.

2. Contravention of the Charity Commission guidelines

The ICA is a Registered Charity (Charity No. 236848, Company No. 444351) and must therefore abide by the Charity Commission guidelines. These guidelines state: "political campaigning, or political activity, as defined in this guidance, must be undertaken by a charity only in the context of supporting the delivery of its charitable purposes."[385]

It seems the Event was "political activity" and therefore the ICA contravened Charity Commission guidelines in as many as two ways: *directly*, by being "political activity", and *indirectly*, by contravening the Memorandum to which the ICA is bound in order to maintain its charitable status. Thus the ICA seems to contravene the Charity Commission guidelines in two ways.

3. Apparent financial impropriety

The Event was hosted and promoted by the ICA and was an official event listed on the ICA website and in press releases. The Event therefore used ICA funds, facilities and staff. The ICA has received funds from the British Council, the Arts Council of England, the National Lottery and other British public bodies, obtained in its capacity as an arts organisation, as set out in the Memorandum.[386] The ICA has received funds from organisations specifically designated to support charities, obtained in its capacity as a Registered Charity. These funds were obtained (respectively) on the grounds that the ICA adhered to its Memorandum as an arts organisation and the guidelines it is bound to follow as a Registered Charity, yet these funds were disbursed on a political campaigning event. Thus the ICA seems to have raised funds to support charitably-designated arts events and disbursed those funds on a political event.

In conclusion, there seem grounds for 1) the ICA to face legal sanctions for contravening the Memorandum, 2) the ICA to face sanctions by the Charity Commission, 3) legal investigation of the ICA for misuse of funds.

I look forward to receiving the ICA's responses to these points.

Yours sincerely

Alexander Adams
Art critic

cc: Charity Commission

cc: The Rt Hon Jeremy Wright MP, Secretary of State for Digital, Culture, Media and Sport; The Rt Hon Tom Watson MP; Commons Select Culture Committee: Damian Collins MP (Chair), Clive Efford MP, Julie Elliott MP, Paul Farrelly MP, Simon Hart MP, Julian Knight MP, Ian C. Lucas MP, Brendan O'Hara MP, Rebecca Pow MP, Jo Stevens MP, Giles Watling MP

14 November 2018

Dear Mr Adams,

I am writing in response to your letter sent to me by post, which I have now received.

In your letter, you suggested that our event, 'Chelsea Manning in conversation with James Bridle', did not further any of the charitable purposes set out in the ICA's governing document.

The ICA's charitable purposes, as set out in our governing document, are *'to promote the education of the community by encouraging the understanding, appreciation and development of the arts generally and particularly of contemporary art as expressed in painting, etching, engraving, drawing, poetry, philosophy, literature, drama, music, opera, ballet, sculpture, architecture, designs, photography, films, radio and television of educational and cultural value'*.

Throughout our 72-year history, as part of our educational role, we have been a site for the development of cultural theory and a place to progress challenging ideas that influence the arts. On its opening at its current location on the Mall on 11 April 1968, the then director of the ICA Michael Kustow remarked that the ICA must be *'a free space, in which the deepest questions that concern us as individuals and society can be explored in continuity […] a sustained enquiry into the roots of our present possibilities and discontents'*. The charitable purposes of the ICA are not simply to present the arts to the public, but also to offer an insight into what drives the development of contemporary art and culture and to enable a better understanding, appreciation and development of the arts through an awareness of the varying contexts in which contemporary art is created.

Over the years, we have hosted a long line of visiting speakers, such as Salman Rushdie, Gyatari Spivak, Roland Barthes, Michel Foucault, Gerry Adams, Vaclav Havel, Toni Morrison and Allen Ginsberg who discussed theories surrounding contemporary culture against a wider backdrop of artistic endeavour. At the ICA, we offer an open forum for this debate to enable reflection and discussion around the wider political, social and economic context in which art is created.

Chelsea Manning was invited to speak to artist James Bridle about topics surrounding the circulation and analysis of data, the media landscape in today's digital age, as well as transgender rights—issues which are of interest to, and inform the work of, many artists who are working today and are crucial to ensuring the advancement of the arts in accordance with the ICA's purposes. These issues have already been considered as part of recent exhibitions at the ICA such as *Counter Investigations* by Forensic Architecture (nominated for the 2018 Turner Prize and currently on view at Tate Britain), our current exhibition by Metahaven entitled *VERSION HISTORY*, Laura Poitras' Academy Award winning documentary *Citizenfour* and the transgender artist Wu Tsang whose work we exhibited in 2015 and who recently won the distinguished $1 Million MacArthur Award. All of the above are artistic practices addressing contemporary issues, such as information democracy, technological developments and transgender rights and Chelsea Manning's experiences and observations were particularly relevant in this context.

The event was not in any way political in nature and any opinions expressed by Chelsea Manning during the talk were not presented as representing the views of the ICA.

In addition, I would like to point out that, to the extent that it is relevant, the Arts Council of England statuary funding represents only 23% of our annual budget, with the balance being raised. Specifically, no public subsidy was directly used to fund this event or its speakers, which was instead made possible through ticket sales and private donations.

Yours sincerely,

Stefan Kalmar
Executive Director

3 December 2018

Dear Mr Kalmar

On 14 November 2018 you responded to concerns over the Chelsea Manning event. You state the event fits a mission to present "cultural theory" and "challenging ideas that influence the arts". Perhaps so, but neither aim conforms to specific articles in the ICA's Memorandum of Association or the ICA's wider purpose to educate regarding the visual arts (again, as set out in the Memorandum). *Even if your stated aims were valid they must be done specifically through presentation or discussion of art, as stipulated by law.* Manning is a political and social campaigner, not a creator and has no expertise in the arts. The conversation, as reported by the ICA and the press, contained no artistic discussion. Therefore it was outside the remit of the Memorandum. Progressing "challenging ideas" includes political campaigning, Chelsea Manning's sole activity. Political-campaigning activity is specifically prohibited by Charity Commission guidelines.

The content and presentation of the event was celebratory; Chelsea Manning was in no way challenged or expected to debate; no contrasting political position was put forward; there was no debate. This event was a platform for Manning's political campaigning, thereby allowing the ICA to use its influence, audience and facilities for political purposes, effectively political campaigning by proxy. Using contextualisation of art as an excuse to justify political campaigning by the ICA is a response which is both inadequate (as any activity could be deemed "contextualisation", rendering the definition meaningless) and irrelevant (as this vague field of activity falls outside legal stipulations applicable).

Raising money from ticket sales and sponsorship is irrelevant. By hosting this event, the ICA used its permanent staff, facilities, website and other resources (funded for arts and charitable ends) for political purposes. The staff who attended the event during working hours were paid and treated as being at work, rather than volunteering for unpaid work on a leave day. The arrangement, execution and promotion for the event were done during the working hours by ICA staff—paid for by taxpayers and donors who thought they were supporting art.

Rather than refuting my objections of 2 October, this response confirms their correctness. The ICA's response is inadequate and disingenuous. It shows that ICA administrators believe their organisation, when it engages in political campaigning, should be immune to regulation and criticism because the causes are morally justified. That is the perfect definition of both elitism and corruption.

Yours sincerely

Alexander Adams
Art critic

B: ICA political campaigning, 2020[387]

On 6 June 2020 the ICA issued a press release illustrated by a photograph of one set of its doors.

> The property relation of the enslaved included and exceeded that of chattel and real estate. Plantation mortgages exemplify the ways in which the value of people who were enslaved, the land they were forced to labor on, and the houses they were forced to maintain were mutually constitutive. Richard Pares writes that "[mortgages] became commoner and commoner until, by 1800, almost every large plantation debt was a mortgage debt." Slaves simultaneously functioned as collateral for

the debts of their masters, while laboring intergenerationally under the debt of the master. The taxation of plantation products imported to Britain, as well as the taxation of interest paid to plantation lenders, provided revenue for Parliament and income for the monarch.

Mahogany became a valuable British import in the 18th century. It was used for a wide variety of architectural applications and furniture, characterizing Georgian and Regency styles. The timbers were felled and milled by slaves in Jamaica, Barbados, and Honduras among other British colonies. It is one of the few commodities of the triangular trade that continues to generate value for those who currently own it.

After taking the throne in 1820, George IV dismantled his residence, Carlton House, and the house of his parents, Buckingham House, combining elements from each to create Buckingham Palace. He built Carlton House Terrace between 1827 and 1832 on the former site of Carlton House as a series of elite rental properties to generate revenue for the Crown. All addresses at Carlton House Terrace are still owned by the Crown Estate, manager of land owned by the Crown since 1760.

12 Carlton House Terrace is leased to the Institute of Contemporary Arts. The building includes four mahogany doors and one mahogany handrail. These five mahogany elements were mortgaged by the Institute of Contemporary Arts to Encumbrance Inc. on January 16th, 2020 for £1000 each. These loans will not be repaid by the ICA. As security for these outstanding debts, Encumbrance Inc. will retain a security interest in these mahogany elements. This interest will constitute an encumbrance on the future transaction of 12 Carlton House Terrace. An encumbrance is a right or interest in real property that does not prohibit its exchange but diminishes its value. The encumbrance will remain on 12 Carlton House Terrace as long as the mahogany elements are part of the building. As reparation, this encumbrance seeks to limit the property's continued accumulation of value for the Crown

Estate. The Crown Estate provides 75% of its revenue to the Treasury and 25% directly to the monarch.
—From the pamphlet for the ICA's current exhibition, Cameron Rowland: 3 & 4 Will. IV c. 73

Stefan Kalmar, Director

In other words, at the behest of a political activist, the ICA has mortgaged leased property. This is illegal. If you rent a property, you have no ownership rights, only usage rights as defined in the tenancy agreement. As an art insider commented: "If it is illegal then it doesn't matter what they think they are achieving, since it would have no validity, and the encumbrance they think they have created would not exist." Amusingly, if the ICA has done what it claimed then they should be liable for eviction and costs pertaining thereto.

The reason the ICA issued this press release in June is because no one had noticed this stunt originally. I—like every art professional I know—did not read this promotional literature this spring. It was just another lengthy harangue by the latest activist invited by the ICA to berate the British public on its complicity in historical crimes.

As I have previously described, the ICA has been taken over by cultural entryists. Once in control of institutions, entryists owe no loyalty towards the organisation, its principles, donors or public. They set their moral vanity above all duty. There is only the holy war of woke: destruction of societal oppression, punishment of hate speech, purging of thought crime. Diversity is not actual diversity; it is relentless onslaught against the majority. For, if the ICA celebrates diversity, why have you not seen promoted by the ICA in the last twenty years any contemporary art even mildly patriotic, pro-family, pro-Christian, pro-Brexit or sceptical about mass migration? Cultural entryists are opportunistic parasites, exploiting taxpayer resources and goodwill.

The director is Stefan Kalmar, someone who spends a fair amount of the year at his home in Berlin. What commitment does an itinerant foreign curator have to the future of a British institution? Once the ICA is destroyed he will move to another node of the global State Art network—something in New York, Barcelona or Montreal—to take up another part-time position, meeting familiar faces at biennales and art fairs. At a lower level, the same will happen to senior staff at the ICA. Why should any of them care?

Senior staff want the ICA to collapse so it can be portrayed as a victim of the establishment. In actuality, the establishment (the mainstream press, MPs, ministers, ACE and Charities Commission England (CCE)) have shielded the ICA from legal consequences or remained silent. It never crossed the minds of ICA staff that announcing illegal actions in press releases would have any consequences because there never have been any. My letters and articles highlighting apparent illegalities were sent directly to MPs, DCMS and CCE; they were ignored. These parties see no harm in illegal activity as long as it aligns with their political sympathies. Like the ICA itself, those who should enforce oversight of the ICA are not held accountable for corruption. Conservative MPs and the government are so terrified of being branded "far right" that they will not intervene to prevent misuse of arts venues/funds by radicals.

Cultural entryists have set the ICA on a course for destruction. They are unable to step back from the cycle of escalation. Driven to satiate their righteous political fury—and having become increasingly irrelevant because of dropping attendance and press coverage—senior ICA staff are taking ever more extreme action. Never checked by internal dissent, never reprimanded by donors, never cautioned by DCMS or ACE, never shamed by the press, the petulant provocateurs of the ICA are driving their father's car ever more recklessly, knowing that if they crash it they will be able to simply walk away without consequences. No senior staff at the ICA will ever be personally prosecuted for ordering illegal acts or bringing down the organisation. They will instead be rewarded with comparable positions at other organisations.

The ICA is beyond saving. It no longer serves a useful function. My recommendations are: 1) The ICA must be liable for diversion of funds for arts purposes into political action. 2) The

ICA must be liable for breaking its Memorandum of Association. 3) The ICA must be liable for refunding to donors misused donations. 4) The ICA must lose its tax-free Registered Charity status for breaking CCE regulations regarding political activity. 5) The ICA must be evicted for breaking the terms of its lease. 6) The ICA must lose all public funding.

C: ICA press releases, 2020

The following are extracts from ICA press releases, grouped by topic.

Race/racism: "In this recorded talk at the ICA, poet and essayist Momtaza Mehri examines black womxn's adoration for cultural and political juggernauts like Beyoncé, Michelle Obama and Oprah. Mehri critiques the limitations of these 'feminist fantasies', pointing instead to figures such as Ella Baker, Claudia Jones and collectives like the Organisation of Women of Asian and African Descent."[388] "[Jeremy O.] Harris made a mark in New York with Slave Play, which examined sex and racial trauma."[389] "Highlighting the emergence of grime as an African diasporic expression[, Cheraine Donalea] Scott explains how grime culture is informed by and responds to issues of race, class and national identity in Brexit Britain."[390] "I have to thank Nana Opoku for introducing me to this 'grassroots TV-esque' project. It offers seven channels of unique content curated by Renata Cherlise, founder of Blvck Vrchives, a submission-based platform featuring photographs from across the African diaspora, and others."[391] "A coalition of US arts workers have come together to confront racism towards diasporic Asians during the pandemic. This website collects testimonies of incidents and provides resources."[392]

Race activism: "If you would like to support the family of George Floyd and the activists and protesters in Minneapolis who are calling for justice, please consider donating to his memorial fund and promoting the work of Black Visions Collective, Reclaim the Block, Unicorn Riot or Take Action Minnesota."[393] "Break into the Forbidden [is an] online fundraiser hosted by Ignota Books is set up to raise money for Black liberation organisations and bail funds in support of resistance movements in the US."[394] "The author of How to Be an Antiracist (2019) talks in Vox's Today Explained series about our individual responsibility for challenging racist policies and power in this podcast."[395] "Francesca Sobande [...] reflects on how Black women and non-binary people resist narratives that seek to portray Europe as 'less racist', and some of the ways regional dynamics in Britain shape the lives of Black people and public discourse concerning racism."[396]

Historical slavery: "A moving short piece from writer M. NourbeSe Philip that considers the present catastrophic moment relative to the catastrophes lived by her ancestors, by those living an enslaved life, as well as by refugees and immigrants."[397]

Feminism: "Devised by Bolanle Tajudeen, founder of Black Blossoms, this course explores how Black women and non-binary artists have challenged their exclusion from the art world by applying DIY approaches and intervening in the social politics of art institutions."[398]

LGBTQ: "This virtual symposium curated by Lilly Markaki reflects on the powers of desire reinvigorated by black, feminist, and queer perspectives."[399] "From 18–24 May, Habibi Collective and ShakoMako present an online short film festival of contemporary queer films from the Middle East and North Africa. The works explore queer identity, sexuality and other aspects of LGBTQ+ experience in the MENA region and among its diaspora, including narratives of 'coming out', cross-dressing, religious oppression, cultural performance and polyamory."[400] "[Eve] Stainton will present their new solo-work Dykegeist at the ICA at a future date—a work that unravels and complicates archetypal and essentialist narratives of lesbian identity."[401] "INFERNO is an incredible community of queers, artists, freaks and weirdos. We're an art platform, a queer techno rave, a community space and a family. INFERNO was a party born out of frustration for London's dwindling gay scene and looking for something more queer and dark."[402]

Transgender issues: "LAVA LAKE is a 24-hour online fundraising event featuring a global line up of 24 QTIBIPOC DJs. This fund has been set up to provide short term support to Queer, Trans and Intersex, Black, Indigenous, People of Colour currently living in the UK who are affected by Covid-19."[403] "ELYLA iz member and founder of da Operación Queer collective formed by Nicaraguan academics, artists and activists in order to create trans-feminist and de-colonial reflections in the Central America region [...]"[404] "Clay AD and Rusti: Dysphoric Feelings / Euphoric Bodies. This workshop is for trans and gender variant people exploring how to understand and work with their dysphoria."[405] "Arists [sic] Raisa Kabir and Raju Rage examine queer health, trans health and ageing in the context of networks of care, disability justice and alternative frameworks for queer survival."[406]

Anti-police: "Another free e-book from Verso—this one by US sociologist Alex S. Vitale, whose recent opinion piece in The Guardian on defunding the police makes a good introduction to this in-depth work on US policing."[407] "Ru & Adam, two organisers from the London Campaign Against Police and State Violence dispel the myth that policing in the UK is not as violent as in the US, unpacking the racist nature of the British police force by contextualising its history in colonial paramilitary policing."[408]

Anti-prisons: "See Something Say Something podcast [is a] series where Ahmed goes into a bit more investigative detail about this underground mango black market; but the episode I really held onto this month was The Honest Struggle, about Islam & incarceration in America. It details between resistance, reform and activism; mass incarceration and the prison industrial complex."[409] "The 4Front Project's [...] work centres on transformative justice and healing whilst directly challenging the UK's addiction to criminalisation, policing and prisons—advocating that racial inequity, the criminal justice system and unaccountability are all drivers of violence."[410]

Anti-Trump: "Here Judith Butler, Maxine Elliot Professor in the Department of Comparative Literature and the Program of Critical Theory at the University of California, Berkeley, tries to make sense of why 70 million US-Americans voted in support of what was essentially a totalitarian takeover attempt (the second highest number of votes for any US candidate ever)."[411]

Anti-Brexit: "Here Benedict Seymour takes Fredric Jameson's 2015 essay 'In Hyperspace' as a starting point to compare the current UK government's Covid-19 and Brexit policies—a device to effect a collective leap into the future, only with the twist that this leap into the 'future' is actually a radical leap into a reactionary past, a rapid leap backwards."[412]

Anarchism: "In conjunction with The Lab, San Francisco, artist and writer Hannah Black here contextualises rent strikes and mutual aid within historical precedents, anarchism and the wider socio-economic implications of the pandemic."[413]

Migration: "Duke University Press: Care in Uncertain Times Syllabus. I am grateful to London artist Erica Scourti for this tip-off, a syllabus on radical care. Perfect for homeschooling, Duke's syllabi series also includes sets on police violence, trans rights and global immigration."[414] "Poet, novelist and anti-racist activist M. NourbeSe Philip is interviewed the day after receiving the 2020 PEN/Nabokov Award for Achievement in International Literature. Philip talks with urgency about the need for a radical hospitality in such times as these."[415] "The publication Recipes for Resistance [...] is part of a wider project that started as a zine, exploring the politics of food and its relationship to culture, coloniality, migration, adaptability and resilience."[416]

Pornography/exhibitionism: "Two years ago we were happy to present the UK premiere of filmmaker Leilah Weintraub's Shakedown, about the Los Angeles black lesbian-owned strip club of the same name. For those who missed it, you can now watch it online at Pornhub [...]"[417] "A transcript and film documentation of a conversation between Samuel R. Delany, Jackie

Wang and Huw Lemmey on the state of public space in relation to cruising, erotic contact and public sex. The conversation responds to the intersections between the city and queer sexual technological practices, neoliberal structured public/private spaces and the historical shifts in the practice of erotic contact. Ultimately, this conversation explores the imaginaries created by public sex and the kinds of socialities it could facilitate."[418]

Sex work: "Radio AvA is both a DIY community radio and a space for sex workers and their allies to reflect, critique, improve safety and celebrate."[419]

Abortion: "Derica Shields presents 'Cleave to the Black: Transcript of a Lecture in Three Parts', an experimental text based on historical, archival and herbal medicine research that attends to the abortive practices of enslaved herbalists, and to the radical embodied epistemologies and value systems that produced them."[420]

Anti-capitalism: "Titans Naomi Klein, Astra Taylor and Keeanga-Yamahtta Taylor strategise on how we can come together to start to counter the greed endemic to social and economic organising powers across the globe."[421] "Mitchell Cowen Verter: Undoing patriarchy, subverting politics: anarchism as a practice of care. [...] This article compellingly explores one of the founding relationships of this political theory, between anarchism and care."[422] "Dean Spade: Solidarity Not Charity: Mutual Aid for Mobilization and Survival. Dean Spade's essay, published in the March issue of Social Text on 'Radical Care' (available for free online), is an essential consideration of mutual aid that offers insights relevant to the current crisis, and to the 'non-natural' disaster of everyday capitalism."[423] "Feminist scholar Anna L. Tsing is a Professor of Anthropology at University of California Santa Cruz and the author of several books including The Mushroom at the End of the World — on the possibilities of life in capitalist ruins."[424] "Alissa Bennett writes incroyable Zines full uh short stories written in her own voice dat are shockingly devastatin in their subject an full of so much stank azz humor an sour insight dat i am mouth open toes curled in deelight when i tear into them. diz iz a saga of uh story Alissa wrote about Barbara Hutton dat i think paints da perfect picture of wtf most of our world is bein run by an headed toward right now which iz MONSTROUS FUKKIN WRETCHED RICH PEEPLE. [sic]"[425]

Anti-colonialism: "After spending several days consuming an excess of information and content related to or inspired by the coronavirus pandemic, finding [Funambulist] podcast has been a breath of fresh air. In each episode, host Leopold Lambert invites a different guest to respond to the same question: 'What is for you a moment of true decolonization?'"[426] "Ariella Aïsha Azoulay is a Palestinian curator, filmmaker and academic who teaches political thought and visual culture at Brown University. Ariella's recent book Potential History: Unlearning Imperialism looks at the imperial origins of our democracies by analysing the technologies that have been developed to support and maintain them."[427] "Curated by Mother Tongues, an interdisciplinary, research-led project that uses decolonial, feminist and queer theory to explore language and identity, this audio series combines music, sounds, poems and thoughts to create a therapeutic soundscape."[428] "The Symposium 'Recursive Colonialism, Artificial Intelligence & Speculative Computation' mixes critical and creative practices, bringing together the philosophy of technology, black studies, political theory, media aesthetics, cultural and digital media studies, and computer science."[429]

Misanthropy: "This short article from our friends at The Guardian includes a lot of useful links to make it clear that the racist narratives emerging now are only employed to divert attention from the real culprit. 70% of all human diseases are caused by direct conflict with animals."[430]

D: Letter to the Charities Commission of England, 2021[431]

30 June 2021

Dear Ms Stephenson[432]

Institute of Contemporary Art, London infraction of CCE regulations

I am writing to draw the CCE's attention to an apparent infraction by a Registered Charity of CCE regulations. On 30 June 2021, the Institute of Contemporary Art, London (Charity No. 236848, Company No. 444351) issued a press release, given in the Appendix. (The information is also available on the ICA website.)[433] The event is a display of material entitled *War Inna Babylon: The Community's Struggle for Truths and Rights*, due to be open from 7 July to 26 September 2021. The press release does not mention art material as being included in the display, which is wholly political/social/legal in content, format and intention, according to the ICA's own admission.[434] Whether this is political campaigning directly or by proxy (allowing political activists to use the ICA as a platform, staff knowing the content of their statements) is a moot point. Political campaigning (direct or by proxy) by the ICA is an infraction of both the ICA Memorandum of Association[435] and prohibited by CCE guidance.[436]

The CCE does not need to take a position on the merits of the display's subject; the action is a contravention of what the ICA is permitted to do as a) an arts venue (according to its own Memorandum) and b) as a Registered Charity. Regardless of what the ICA or its clients may say, the majority of the British population do not regard political activity as art. Indeed, making distinctions between campaigning material and art is vital for the survival of the current arts-funding structure as it permits arts organisations to resist being parasitised by activists (regardless of political outlook).

As per my previous letter copied to the CCE (2 October 2018) and my submission of evidence to Parliament Select Committee (9 March 2020), CCE will be aware that the ICA has repeatedly abused its position as a Registered Charity to engage in political campaigning. As such, the ICA has a persistent behaviour of flouting regulations and apparently diverting funds received on the basis a) that the ICA is a Registered Charity (despite breaching CCE guidance) and b) that the ICA will use donations (including substantial donations from public bodies) solely for the promotion of art. This makes the new infraction not an aberration but part of a years-long campaign abusing its position as an arts venue with Registered Charity status in order to satisfy the personal political agendas of staff. The matter of whether any financial regulations have been broken (i.e. the apparent diversion of donations intended for artistic projects being used for political campaigning) is a matter for other authorities, including Department of Digital, Culture, Media and Sport, to which this letter is being copied.

Considering the multiple infractions of no-political-campaigning CCE guidance which have been committed by the ICA over many years, I urge the CCE to sanction the ICA by withdrawing its status as a Registered Charity. The impartiality of charity arts organisations, the resistance of arts organisations to political takeovers and public trust in the funding of arts venues are all at stake.

Yours sincerely

Alexander Adams
Art critic

cc: Oliver Dowden MP, Secretary for State, DCMS; ICA, London
[*Enclosed ICA press release omitted*]

About the authors

Alexander Adams is a British artist and writer. He studied art at Goldsmiths College, London. His art has been exhibited worldwide and is in the collections of the Victoria & Albert Museum, National Museum of Wales, Walker Art Gallery and other museums. His art criticism has been published in *The Art Newspaper*, *The Critic*, *The Jackdaw* and other outlets. His poetry has been published in anthologies, broadsides and single-author volumes in the UK and USA. Alexander Adams is the recipient of the 2018 Artist Scholarship from the Francis Bacon MB Art Foundation, Monaco. He lives in England.

Michael Sandle, SRA, was born in Weymouth, Dorset, in 1936. He grew up in Douglas, Isle of Man. He studied fine art at Douglas School of Art and Technology (1951–54) and the Slade School of Fine Art, London (1956–59). Following his appointment as professor of sculpture at Pforzheim, Germany, in 1973, and at Karlsruhe, Germany, in 1980, Sandle's work became more monumental, partly in response to a series of significant commemorative commissions. His work voices criticisms of what Sandle describes as "the heroic decadence" of capitalism, in particular its appetite for global conflict. He has also attacked the media for packaging and sanitising the destructiveness of war. He has had a stormy relationship with the Royal Academy, having resigned in 1997 as an RA but agreed to rejoin in 2004. He is now a Senior Academician. In 1994 he was elected Fellow of the Royal Society of British Sculptors. He is currently the patron of the Public Statues and Sculpture Association. He has exhibited in numerous group exhibitions in Britain and internationally including the 5th Paris Biennale, 4th and 6th Documenta and São Paulo Biennale. His work is in major art institutions, including the British Museum, Metropolitan Museum and Australian National Museum. The work he is most proud of is the Malta WW2 Siege Memorial, which stands at the entrance to the Grand Harbour,

Valletta, and for which the National Sculpture Society of America awarded him the Henry Hering Medal.

Textual history

Parts of this book were previously published in different forms. Appendix A was first published in as "ICA and Politics" in *The Jackdaw*, no. 143, January/February 2019. Appendix B was first published as "ICA, Artivism and Illegality" in *The Jackdaw*, no. 152, July/August 2020. Appendix C comprises press releases of the ICA compiled by the author, some republished in multiple issues of *The Jackdaw*. The letter and press releases from the ICA are in the public domain. The main text includes writing published in *The Critic*, *The Jackdaw*, *Bournbrook Magazine*, *Spiked Online* and www.alexanderadamsart.wordpress.com.

Acknowledgements

I would like to thank Michael Sandle for his generous foreword. I have long been an admirer of his art and personal integrity and am honoured to receive his (tempered) endorsement. I would like to also to thanks David Lee, Michael Curzon, Tim Black, Robin Simon, Michael Mosbacher, Olivia Hartley, Selby Whittingham, Michael Daley, Theodore Dalrymple, Edward Lucie-Smith, Charles Thomson, Ella Guru, Andrew Bledsoe, Erin Hemmer, my mother and contributors, advisors and interviewees who prefer to remain anonymous. None of the contributors necessarily share the author's opinions; errors and omissions are entirely the author's.

Bibliography

Hans Abbing, *Why Are Artists Poor? The Exceptional Economy of the Arts*, Amsterdam University Press, 2014

Alexander Adams, *Culture War: Art, Identity Politics and Cultural Entryism*, Societas/Imprint Academic, 2019

Alexander Adams, *Iconoclasm: Identity Politics and the Erasure of History*, Societas/Imprint Academic, 2020

Sohrab Ahmari, *The New Philistines: How Identity Politics Disfigure the Arts*, Biteback, 2016

Ruaridh Arrow, *Gene Sharp: How to Start a Revolution*, The Big Indy Books, 2020

Sascia Bailer, Magdalena Kallenberger, Maicyra Leão Teles e Silva (eds.), *Re-Assembling Motherhood(s): On Radical Care and Collective Art as Feminist Practices*, Onomatopee, 2021

Tabitha Barber, Stacy Boldrick (eds.), *Art Under Attack: Histories of British Iconoclasm*, Tate, 2013

Banksy, *Wall and Piece*, Century, 2006

Kathy Battista, *New York, New Wave: The Legacy of Feminist Art in Emerging Practice*, I.B. Tauris, 2019

James Burnham, *The Machiavellians: Defenders of Freedom*, Lume Books, 2020

James Burnham, *The Managerial Revolution: What is Happening in the World*, Lume Books, 2021

James Burnham, *Suicide of the West: An Essay on the Meaning and Destiny of Liberalism*, Encounter Books, 2014

Teresa A. Carbone, Kellie Jones, *Witness: Art and Civil Rights in the Sixties*, Brooklyn Museum/The Monacelli Press, 2014

Whitney Chadwick, *Women, Art, and Society*, fifth edition, Thames & Hudson, 2012

Herschel B. Chipp (*ed.*), *Theories of Modern Art*, University of California Press, 1968

Alex Danchev (*ed.*), *100 Artists' Manifestos from the Futurists to the Stuckists*, Penguin Books, 2011

Katy Deepwell (*ed.*), *Feminist Art Activisms and Artivisms*, Valiz, 2020

Marilyn Delaure, Moritz Fink (*eds.*), *Culture Jamming: Activism and the Art of Cultural Resistance*, New York University Press, 2017

John Dewey, *Art as Experience*, Capricorn Books, 1934

Antony Easthope, Kate McGowan (*eds.*), *A Critical and Cultural Theory Reader*, Open University Press, 2004

Will Ellsworth-Jones, *Banksy: The Man Behind the Wall*, Aurum, 2012

Eva Etzioni-Halevy, *The Elite Connection: Problems and Potential of Western Democracy*, Polity Press, 1993

Clare Farrell, Alison Green, Sam Knights, William Skeaping (*eds.*), *This is not a Drill: An Extinction Rebellion Handbook*, Penguin, 2019

Vivien Green Fryd, *Against Our Will: Sexual Trauma in American Art Since 1970*, Pennsylvania State University Press, 2019

Matthew Fuller, Eyal Weizman, *Investigative Aesthetics: Conflicts and Commons in the Politics of Truth*, Verso, 2021

Charles Harrison, Paul Wood, Jason Gaiger (*eds.*), *Art in Theory, 1815–1900*, Blackwell, 2001

Charles Harrison, Paul Wood (*eds.*), *Art in Theory, 1900–2000*, Blackwell, 2003

Eleanor Heartney, Helaine Posner, Nancy Princenthal, Sue Scott, *The Reckoning: Women Artists of the New Millennium*, Prestel, 2013

Pablo Helguera, *Education for Socially Engaged Art*, Jorge Pinto Books, 2011

Jeffrey H. Jackson, *Paper Bullets: Two Artists Who Risked Their Lives to Defy the Nazis*, Algonquin Books, 2020

Angus Kennedy, *Being Cultured: In Defence of Discrimination*, Societas/Imprint Academic, 2014

Grant H. Kester (*ed.*), *Art, Activism & Oppositionality: Essays from Afterimage*, Duke University Press, 1998

Adam Michael Krause, *Art as Politics: The Future of Art and Community*, New Compass Press, 2011

Gaetano Mosca, *The Ruling Class*, McGraw-Hill Book Company, 1939
Arcadi Poch, Daniela Poch, *Artivism*, Carpet Bombing Culture, 2018
Maura Reilly, *Curatorial Activism: Towards an Ethics of Curating*, Thames & Hudson, 2019
Roger Scruton, *Beauty: A Very Short Introduction*, Oxford University Press, 2011
Jennifer L. Shaw, *Exist Otherwise: The Life and Works of Claude Cahun*, Reaktion Books, 2017
Gregory Sholette, *Delirium and Resistance: Activist Art and the Crisis of Capitalism*, Pluto Press, 2017
Thomas Sowell, *The Vision of the Anointed*, Basic Books, 1995
Nato Thompson, *Seeing Power: Art and Activism in the 21st Century*, Melville House, 2015
Steve Wright, *Banksy's Bristol: Home Sweet Home*, Tangent Books, 2009

Essays, theses, reports, research papers

Anonymous, *Public perceptions of – and attitudes to – the purposes of museums in society: A report prepared by BritainThinks for Museum Association*, BritainThinks, March 2013
Anonymous, *Museums as Economic Engines: A National Report*, American Alliance of Museums, December 2017
Anonymous, *IPSOS MORI Veracity Index*, IPSOS, November 2020
Asunción Bernárdez Rodal, Graciela Padilla Castillo, Roxana Popelka Sosa Sánchez, "From Action Art to Artivism on Instagram: Relocation and instantaneity for a new geography of protest", *Catalan Journal of Communication & Cultural Studies*, vol. 11, no. 1, 2019, pp. 23–37
Adrienne Callander, "Artmaking as Entrepreneurship: Effectuation and Emancipation in Artwork Formation", *Artivate*, Summer 2019, Vol. 8, No. 2 (Summer 2019), pp. 61–77
Consilium Research & Consultancy, *Equality and Diversity within the Arts and Cultural Sector in England, Evidence and Literature Review, Final Report*, Arts Council of England, undated (2014)
Gail Gallagher, "Art, Activism and the Creation of Awareness of Missing and Murdered Indigenous Women and Girls (MMIWG); Walking With Our Sisters, REDress Project", University of Alberta, 2020

Bibliography

Martin Gilens, Benjamin I. Page, "Testing Theories of American Politics: Elites, Interest Groups, and Average Citizens", Cambridge University Press, 18 September 2014

Alistair Hudson, "An institution that works on visitors' terms", *The Museums Journal*, June 2019, p. 19

Kabir Jhala, "Manchester gallery accused of provoking racial discord over exhibition on environmental effects of Israel-Palestine conflict", *The Art Newspaper*, 12 August 2021 [accessed 14 August 2021].

Allan Kaprow, "The Education of the Un-Artist, Part 1", 1971

Tilia Korpe, "Artivism in Tunis Music and Art as tools of creative resistance & the cultural re: mixing of a revolution", Malmö Högskola, 2013

Lucy Lippard, "The Art Workers' Coalition: Not a History", *Studio International*, November 1970

Lucy Lippard, "Trojan Horses: Activist Art and Power", 1984

Jeremy Liu, Victor Rubin, "Social Cohesion that Advances Equity and WellBeing: Promising Practices in Community Development, Health, and the Arts", April 2021

Herbert Marcuse, "Repressive Tolerance", 1965

Anna Matejcek, "Influence: Art, Activism, and Identity as Seen Through a Neurodivergent Lens", Boise State University, May 2017

Sarah Mekdjian, "Urban artivism and migrations. Disrupting spatial and political segregation of migrants in European cities", 23 June 2017

Chiara Dalle Nogare, Raffaele Scuderi, Enrico E. Bertacchini, "Museums' commitment to immigrant integration: A quantitative analysis", undated

Sonali Pahwa, Jessica Winegar, "Culture, State and Revolution", 2012

Leslie Robinson "Becoming Artivists: Artivist Inter-Actions Toward Creative Re-Existence", University of Alberta, 2015

Alan Tomlinson, *Mental Health and Visual Arts*, What Works Centre for Wellbeing, January 2018

Tom Wilson, Richard Walton, *Extremism Rebellion: A review of ideology and tactics*, Policy Exchange, July 2019

United Nations, *Creative Economy Report 2010*, 2010

Documentaries

Graffiti Wars, Channel 4, documentary, 2011
Exit Through the Gift Shop, Rex Features, documentary, 2010

Endnotes

1. Poch and Poch, 2018, p. 9.
2. See Appendix A.
3. See Appendix B.
4. "Another free e-book from Verso—this one by US sociologist Alex S. Vitale, whose recent opinion piece in The Guardian on defunding the police makes a good introduction to this in-depth work on US policing" (ICA press release, 2 June 2020).
5. ICA press release, 2 June 2020.
6. Zarina Muhammed: "Kashmir has been locked down by the Indian military since last August when the Indian government revoked Kashmir's special status and stripped it of a long-held constitutional autonomy. There's a media blackout, no internet, phone lines have been cut, roads are blocked, there are shootings and repeated violence from the Indian army; it's imposing direct rule from Delhi, and it is an act of extreme state violence from a state that's currently being run by an openly islamophobic, Hindu nationalist government" (ICA press release, 1 June 2021).
7. See above and Appendix C.
8. ICA press release, 17 December 2019.
9. ICA press release, 6 November 2020.
10. ICA press release, 1 May 2020.
11. See Adams, 2020, pp. 97–9, and Alexander Adams, "The Colston Statue Affair", *The Jackdaw*, no. 153, September/October 2020, pp. 10–1.
12. ICA press release, 9 June 2020.
13. David Goodhart, *The Road to Somewhere*, Hurst, 2017.
14. See Appendix A.
15. ICA press release, 30 June 2021.
16. ICA press release, 30 June 2021.
17. See Appendix D.
18. Dalya Alberge, "Artist claims ICA race show breaks rules about politics", *The Sunday Telegraph*, 4 July 2021, p. 7.
19. See Adams (2019, pp. 106–42).
20. https://artreview.netlify.app/stefan-kalmar-to-leave-london-institute-of-contemporary-arts-ica/ [accessed 11 August 2021].
21. *The Art Newspaper*, 11 August 2021.
22. James Noyes, *The Politics of Iconoclasm: Religion, Violence and the Culture of Image-Breaking in Christianity and Islam*, I.B. Tauris, 2016, p. 24.
23. Jeremy D. Popkin, *A New World Begins: The History of the French Revolution*, Basic Books, 2019, p. 352.

24 See Bruno Chenique (*ed.*), *Géricault: Images of Life and Death*, Hirmer, 2013.
25 Vladimir Mayakovsky, "Manifesto of the Flying Federation of Futurists", 1918, in Danchev, 2011, pp. 134–5.
26 See also the parallel contemporaneous movement of the Bauhaus, with its radical inter-disciplinary character and applied-fine art fusion.
27 Andrei Zhadanov, "Speech to the Congress of Soviet Writers", 1932, in Harrison and Wood, 2003, p. 428.
28 "The simplest Surrealist act consists of dashing down into the street, pistol in hand, and firing blindly, as fast as you can pull the trigger, into the crowd. Anyone who has not dreamed of thus putting an end to the petty system of debasement and cretinization in effect has a well-defined place in the crowd with his belly at barrel level." Breton, quoted Richard Wolin, *The Seduction of Unreason*, Princeton University Press, 2nd edition, 2019, p. 181.
29 On 22 January 1923 a young anarchist, Germaine Berton, assassinated Marius Plateau, journalist and secretary of the Ligue d'Action française, the ultra-nationalist Catholic political group. The Surrealists sent a bouquet to Berton when she was acquitted of the murder.
30 For Surrealist support for murderess Violette Nozière, see esp. Sarah Maza, *Violette Nozière: A Story of Murder in 1930s Paris*, University of California Press, 2011.
31 Guy Debord, "Situationist Manifesto", 1960, in Danchev, 2011, p. 350.
32 Marco Evaristti offered visitors a chance to activate a food blender which had a live goldfish in water inside it, Denmark, 2000. The blender was activated at least once, killing two fish. A Danish court ruled that the act was not a crime of cruelty against animals. Various sources.
33 https://www.foundsf.org/index.php?title=Legacy_of_the_Neighborhood_Arts_Program [accessed 14 August 2021].
34 Judithe Hernández, interview, 28 March 1998: https://www.aaa.si.edu/collections/interview-judithe-hernandez-6345#transcript [accessed 2 August 2021].
35 *Ibid.*
36 Trend, "Cultural Struggle and Educational Activism", in Kester, 1998, p. 174.
37 Quoted in Trend, "Cultural Struggle and Educational Activism", in Kester, 1998, p. 175.
38 https://acdarchives.blogspot.com/ [accessed 14 August 2021].
39 Lippard, 1970.
40 https://www.democraticcomm.org/about [accessed 14 August 2021].
41 Lucy Lippard, "Sweeping Exchanges: The Contribution of Feminism to the Art of the 1970s", *Art Journal*, Fall-Winter 1980, p. 362.
42 Whitney Chadwick & Isabelle de Courtivron (*eds.*), *Significant Others:*

Creativity & Intimate Partnership, Thames & Hudson, 1993, p. 10.
43   Katy Deepwell in Deepwell, 2020, p. 12.
44   *Ibid.*, p. 11.
45   *Ibid.*, p. 11–12.
46   *Ibid.*, p. 13.
47   See Adams, 2019, pp. 96–7.
48   See Kokoli in Deepwell, 2020.
49   "If we are to leave the masculinist, white supremacist model behind once and for all, a completely different way of understanding art and how artmaking is related to everything else is required. The science of ecology provides metaphors that help visualize the potential for this." Alana Jelinek, "Feminist Artivisms" in Deepwell, 2020, p. 218.
50   Helena Reckitt (*ed.*), *The Art of Feminism: Images that Shaped the Fight for Equality*, Tate, 2019, p. 188.
51   A feminist performance artist I knew used to wear a T-shirt with the word "cunt" written on it. She would interpret looks of disapproval and negative comments not as expressions of discomfort or objections to public profanity but as indications of widespread revulsion regarding female anatomy and as an attempt to silence women's speech. She framed responses to her provocation as attacks; this allowed her to consider herself a victim.
52   https://occupythekitchen.org/Food-Artivism [accessed 1 August 2021].
53   http://www.foodjustice.org/team [accessed 1 August 2021].
54   Matejcek, 2017, p. vi.
55   Gallagher, 2020, p. 13.
56   *Ibid.*, p. 10.
57   *Ibid.*, p. 12.
58   Robinson, 2015, p. iv.
59   *Ibid.*, p. iiii.
60   Aline Fantinatti, 1 August 2021, https://www.redumbrellafund.org/artivism/ [accessed 2 August 2021].
61   This section is largely drawn from Jackson, 2020, and Shaw, 2017.
62   Shaw, 2017, p. 82.
63   *Ibid.*, p. 96.
64   See Julius von Schlosser, *Art and Curiosity Cabinets of the Late Renaissance*, Getty Research Institute, 2021.
65   Consolidated Royal Charter, 31 May 1994, p. 2.
66   *Ibid.*, p. 2.
67   https://web.archive.org/web/20060901102346/http://www.nea.gov/about/index.html [accessed 14 August 2021].
68   Grant H. Kester, "Alternative Arts Sector and the Imaginary Public", in Kester, 1998, pp. 105–9.

69 For the NEA protection of non-commercial artists, see Grant H. Kester, "Alternative Arts Sector and the Imaginary Public", in Kester, 1998, p. 116.
70 For the politics of the Roosevelt administration's Works Projects Administration in the 1930s, see Jody Patterson, *Modernism for the Masses: Painters, Politics, and Public Murals in 1930s New York*, Yale University Press, 2020.
71 Grant H. Kester, "Alternative Arts Sector and the Imaginary Public", in Kester, 1998, pp. 104–5.
72 Grant H. Kester, "Ongoing Negotiations", in Kester, 1998, pp. 1–19.
73 Patrick Buchanan (1989): "While the right has been busy winning primaries and elections, cutting taxes, and funding anticommunist guerrillas abroad, the left has been quietly seizing all the commanding heights of American art and culture." Quoted in Trend, "Cultural Struggle and Educational Activism", in Kester, 1998, p. 171.
74 For the pre-emptive censorship of the Hans Bellmer exhibition, 2007, London, see Alexander Adams, "Pre-emptive Censorship", *The Jackdaw*, no. 75, February 2008, p. 12.
75 Advocates even admit the class divide between (on one hand) the producers and creators on artivism and (on the other hand) the working-class participants-cum-subjects, which generates friction over what is "art" and what is "useful". See Helguera, 2011, esp. p. 23.
76 Anthony Kenny, *A History of Western Philosophy*, Oxford University Press, 2012, p. 928.
77 "The idea of museums reaching out into communities or sections of societies isn't one that the public sees them as being the best placed to do", BritainThinks, 2013, p. 5.
78 "Those that participants did not see as sitting easily with the essential purposes of museums", roles that "undermined the essential values of trust and integrity that people cherish with regards to museums", BritainThinks, 2013, p. 6.
79 BritainThinks, 2013, pp. 4–6.
80 https://www.britishcouncil.org/voices-magazine/museums-can-play-role-urban-regeneration [accessed 15 August 2021].
81 https://www.moma.org/explore/inside_out/2010/03/15/my-life-in-museums-the-importance-of-community-outreach-and-teen-programs/ [accessed 15 August 2021].
82 https://www.tandfonline.com/doi/abs/10.1080/0161956X.2011.561171?journalCode=hpje20 [accessed 15 August 2021].
83 Liu and Rubin, 2021, p. 1.
84 https://ccrweb.ca/en/speak-up/reclaim-honour-stories [accessed 19 August 2021].
85 Nogare et al., p. 2.
86 https://www.statista.com/topics/1509/museums/ [acessed 15 August

2021].
87 "Museums as Economic Engines", p. 5.
88 https://www.futuremarketinsights.com/reports/museum-tourism-sector-overview [accessed 15 August 2021].
89 Kennedy, 2014.
90 *Ibid.*, p. 7
91 Tomlinson, 2018, p. 3.
92 *Ibid.*, p. 8.
93 Press release, 13 May 2021. Accessed 13 May 2021.
94 Press release, National Gallery, London, 30 July 2021. Accessed 30 July 2021.
95 "She has also garnered enormous admiration as an artist who overcame strongly adverse circumstances—a motherless household, rape at the hands of a colleague of her father's, a forced loveless marriage, the death of all but one of her children, and constant financial difficulties—to become a great history painter", Elizabeth Cropper, in Letizia Treves (*ed.*) *Artemisia*, National Gallery, 2020, p. 7.
96 Korpe, 2013, p. 12.
97 George Orwell, "The Frontiers of Art and Propaganda", 1941.
98 *Ibid.*
99 https://www.colleendilen.com/2017/04/26/people-trust-museums-more-than-newspapers-here-is-why-that-matters-right-now-data/ [accessed 1 August 2021].
100 IPSOS MORI, 2020, p. 2.
101 "Those who had not visited a museum in that time were less likely to believe that a museum should have something to say about social issues, with just 21% stating that they should. This increase[d] to 27% when someone had visited 1–2 times, 35% when someone had visited 3–4 times, 37% when someone had visited 5–6 times and 39.5% when someone had been to a museum more than 6 times in the past 12 months", https://www.museumnext.com/article/should-museums-be-activists/ [accessed 1 August 2021].
102 *Ibid.*
103 The managerial elite is distinct from a common concept, Mencius Moldbug's "Cathedral": "the general left-liberal consensus among the establishment in the modern West" (https://www.arimathea.org/j/p/more_on_moldbugs_cathedral [accessed 15 August 2021]). "'The cathedral' is just a short way to say 'journalism plus academia'—in other words, the intellectual institutions at the center of modern society, just as the Church was the intellectual institution at the center of medieval society" (https://graymirror.substack.com/p/a-brief-explanation-of-the-cathedral [accessed 15 August 2021]). "The Cathedral, with its informal union of

church and state, is positioned perfectly. It has all the advantages of being a formal arm of government, and none of the disadvantages. Because it formulates public policy, it is best considered our ultimate governing organ, but it certainly bears no responsibility for the success or failure of said policy" (Moldbug, *A Gentle Introduction to Unqualified Reservations, Unqualified Reservations,* 2015).

104 *Ibid.*
105 https://www.colleendilen.com/2019/03/06/in-museums-we-trust-heres-how-much-data-update/ [accessed 1 August 2021].
106 Anthony Kenny, *A History of Western Philosophy,* Oxford University Press, 2012, p. 958.
107 "[… T]here are always, in fact, restrictions about the limits of democratically acceptable opposition. When the minority goes beyond these limits it is not given rights to propagate its views but suppressed as 'subversive' or 'criminal' or 'vicious'", Burnham, 2021, p. 152.
108 Banksy, 2006, p. 95. Banksy has admitted in an interview his debt to 1980s Paris street artist Blek le Rat, who stencilled rats and figures in political wall art. Blek feels ambivalent about fathering a style that has become a worldwide money-spinner without receiving more than incidental acknowledgement. Source: *Graffiti Wars.*
109 Banksy, 2006, p. 13.
110 Ellsworth-Jones, 2012, p. 57.
111 *Ibid.,* caption.
112 *Ibid.,* p. 169.
113 Another double-printing listed Ellsworth-Jones, 2012, p. 186.
114 *Ibid.,* pp. 181–204 and throughout.
115 Benedikt Feiten, "Answering Back!", in Delaure and Fink, 2017, p. 219.
116 "1974", Wright, 2009, p. 32; "1973", various sources.
117 Ellsworth-Jones, 2012, p. 32.
118 Banksy, 2006, Wright, 2009, Ellsworth-Jones, 2012.
119 Throughout Wright, 2009.
120 Quoted Wright, 2009, p. 5.
121 *Exit Through the Gift Shop.*
122 Ellsworth-Jones, 2012, p. 1.
123 *Ibid.,* p. 105.
124 Throughout Ellsworth-Jones, 2012.
125 For the ineffectiveness of electoral democracy, see Etzioni-Halevy, 1993, pp. 23–4.
126 See Mancur Olson, *The Logic of Collective Action: Public Goods and the Theory of Groups,* Harvard University Press, 1971.
127 Mosca, 1939, p. 56.
128 George Orwell, "Second Thoughts on James Burnham", 1946.

[129] Burnham, 2021, p. 84.
[130] *Ibid.*, p. 108.
[131] George Orwell, "Second Thoughts on James Burnham", 1946.
[132] Subsidisation of film-television production by individual US states: https://web.archive.org/web/20200917023212/https://www.latimes.com/opinion/la-xpm-2011-mar-01-la-oe-kinsley-column-movie-subsidies-20110301-story.html [accessed 3 August 2021].
[133] Disney gaining copyright-protection law extension: https://www.theiplawblog.com/2016/02/articles/copyright-law/disneys-influence-on-united-states-copyright-law/ [accessed 3 August 2021].
[134] Covid-19 vaccine manufacturers granted immunity from prosecution: https://www.newsweek.com/fact-check-are-pharmaceutical-companies-immune-covid-19-vaccine-lawsuits-1562793 [accessed 3 August 2021].
[135] US federal government working through Twitter for emergency alerts: https://www.govtech.com/public-safety/governments-use-twitter-for-emergency-alerts.html [accessed 3 August 2021].
[136] US federal government $80.7bn bailout for the motor industry: https://www.thebalance.com/auto-industry-bailout-gm-ford-chrysler-3305670 [accessed 3 August 2021].
[137] See Burnham, 2021, pp. 95–101.
[138] Burnham, 2020, p. 205.
[139] "*If* the process [of contraction] continues over the next decades just past, *then* – this is a merely mathematical extrapolation – the West will be finished […] It may be added that suicide [of nations] is probably more frequent than murder [of nations] as the end phase of a civilisation", Burnham, 2014, p. 14.
[140] "Defined as wielders of power and influence on the basis of their control of resources […] Elites include the political elite (of the government and opposition), the business elite, the elite of trade unions and of the media, as well as some others […]", Etzioni-Halevy, 1993, p. 9.
[141] "[… Marxist] class theory came to be regarded as progressive, egalitarian and democratic, while elite theory has come to be regarded as conservative, elitist, inegalitarian and undemocratic", *ibid.*, p. 28.
[142] *Ibid.*, p. 43.
[143] *Ibid.*, p. 29.
[144] *Ibid.*, pp. 8–9.
[145] *Ibid.*, p. 104.
[146] *Ibid.*, p. 6.
[147] *Ibid.*, p. 95.
[148] *Ibid.*, p. 209.
[149] Consilium, 2014, p. 46.
[150] "Arts organisations among best employers for women", *Arts Professional*, 6

April 2018, https://www.artsprofessional.co.uk/news/arts-organisations-among-best-employers-women [retrieved 21 May 2019].
151 "Arts organisations reveal their gender pay gaps", *Arts Professional*, 16 March 2018, https://www.artsprofessional.co.uk/news/arts-organisations-reveal-their-gender-pay-gaps [retrieved 21 May 2019]; "65.7%", Arts Council of England, *Annual Report 2018-9*, p. 72.
152 2018, Kate McMillan, "Representation of women artists in Britain during 2018", *Freelands Foundation*, May 2019, p. 5.
153 The percentage of women in US museum administration went from 59% in 2015 to 61% in 2018. Of curator positions, 74% were held by women in 2018. Mariët Westermann, Roger Schonfeld and Liam Sweeney, *Art Museum Demographic Survey 2018*, Andrew W. Mellon Foundation, 28 January 2019, pp. 7-8.
154 81.6% of women (75.1% of men). Consilium, 2014, p. 43.
155 53% of women, 52.5% of men. Consilium, 2014, p. 43.
156 Consilium, 2014, p. 52.
157 "96% of the UK's Creative Industries Federation members were against leaving the EU", Gesa Stedman and Sandra van Lente (eds.) *It's Not Just the Economy, Stupid! Brexit and the Cultural Sector*, Literary Field Kaleidoscope and the Centre for British Studies Humboldt-Universität zu Berlin, 2017, p. 8.
158 Labour: 53% opposed Brexit, 20% supported. Compared to Lib Dem: 70/12; Con.: 29/60; left-identifying: 66/10; centre: 35/39; right: 35/48. https://www.pewresearch.org/fact-tank/2019/10/28/brexit-divides-the-uk-but-partisanship-and-ideology-are-still-key-factors/ [accessed 30 July 2021].
159 https://www.bbc.co.uk/news/uk-politics-eu-referendum-35616946 [accessed 31 July 2021].
160 https://www.dezeen.com/2016/05/20/heatherwick-chipperfield-adjaye-architects-designers-creatives-opposing-brexit-remain-european-union-referendum/ and https://www.theguardian.com/politics/2016/may/19/british-cultural-heavyweights-sign-250-letter-backing-eu-benedict-cumberbatch-paloma-faith- [accessed 31 July 2021].
161 https://www.dezeen.com/2016/06/16/90-per-cent-british-fashion-council-designers-oppose-leave-brexit-support-remain-european-union-eu-referendum/ [accessed 31 July 2021].
162 https://www.theguardian.com/technology/2016/mar/04/britains-tech-sector-overwhelmingly-opposed-to-brexit [accessed 31 July 2021].
163 https://www.theatlantic.com/international/archive/2016/06/uk-brexit-guide/482730/ [accessed 31 July 2021].
164 "[... O]nly 23% of contributors in the programmes as a whole spoke in favour of Brexit, against 58% in favour of Remain and 19% who gave a

neutral or factual commentary", http://news-watch.co.uk/bbc-brexit-collection-strong-bias-against-leaving-the-eu/ [accessed 30 July 2021].
165 Remi Adekoya, Eric Kaufmann and Thomas Simpson, *Academic Freedom in the UK*, Policy Exchange, 2020, p. 7.
166 https://www.aei.org/articles/are-colleges-and-universities-too-liberal-what-the-research-says-about-the-political-composition-of-campuses-and-campus-climate/ [accessed 31 July 2021].
167 2018, Cornell University, https://cornellsun.com/2018/11/05/99-5-cornell-faculty-academics-donations-given-to-left-leaning-groups/ [accessed 31 July 2021].
168 Remi Adekoya, Eric Kaufmann and Thomas Simpson, *Academic Freedom in the UK*, Policy Exchange, 2020, p. 7.
169 Arts: 79.5% of whites, 70% of blacks. Museums: 53.7%/45%. Consilium, 2014, p. 33.
170 https://www.statista.com/statistics/1096448/ethnic-diversity-in-creative-industries-in-the-uk-by-sector/ [accessed 21 July 2021].
171 Consilium, 2014, p. 67.
172 Burnham on Western liberals at the top of society (in the 1960s) who downplay the decline of the West: "[Western liberals] hate their own civilization, readily excuse or even praise blows struck against it, and themselves lend a willing hand, frequently enough, to pulling it down", Burnham, 2014, p. 14.
173 https://www.dailymail.co.uk/news/article-8086771/Nearly-half-Labor-members-ashamed-countrys-history-new-poll-reveals.html [accessed 21 July 2021].
174 Sowell notes certain acceptable targets for the elite ("the anointed"), namely business and the professions, the family and religion. Sowell, 1995, pp. 168–82. I slightly differ, seeing in the professions a cadre of the experts (tactically used to provide arguments supporting policies) who both comprise the technocratic managerial elite and are used by that elite.
175 Burnham detected what he called a "liberal" consensus at the top level of American society. "The predominant assumptions, ideas and beliefs about politics, economics, and social questions are liberal. I do not mean that a large majority of the population is, by count, liberal. Perhaps a majority is liberal, but that is hard to determine accurately. What is certain is that a majority, and a substantial majority, of those who control or influence public opinion is liberal, that liberalism of one or another variety prevails among the opinion-makers, molders and transmitters […]", Burnham, 2014, p. 22. On liberal consensus and conformity, Burnham, 2014, pp. 17–37.
176 Abbing, 2014, p. 225.
177 *Ibid.*

[178] Kaprow, 1971.
[179] Callander, 2019, p. 69.
[180] Poch and Poch, 2018, pp. 28-30.
[181] *Ibid.*, p. 28.
[182] Doris Salcedo, "Interview", 1999, in Harrison and Wood, 2003, pp. 1182-3.
[183] Poch and Poch, 2018, pp. 10-7.
[184] Heartney and Posner, 2013, p. 204.
[185] Christine Harold, "Pranking Rhetoric", in Delaure and Fink, 2017, p. 65.
[186] Marco Deseriis, "The Faker as Producer", in Delaure and Fink, 2017, p. 102.
[187] Christine Harold, "Pranking Rhetoric", in Delaure and Fink, 2017, pp. 77-80.
[188] Adams, 2020, pp. 83-5.
[189] "[… L]iberals differ, or may differ, among themselves on application, timing, method and other details, but those differences revolve within a common framework of more basic ideas, beliefs, principles, goals, feelings and values", Burnham, 2014, p. 29.
[190] Paolo Ruffino et al., "Art, Authority, and Culture Jamming", in Delaure and Fink, 2017, pp. 428-9.
[191] Maik Fielitz and Reem Ahmed, "It's not funny any more. The far-right extremists' use of humour", Publications Office of the European Union, August 2021.
[192] *Ibid.*, p. 14.
[193] "[Aims include 1.] Ending biosphere destruction and working towards its regeneration by abandoning dangerous conceptions of pseudo-abundance in the natural world (based on the assumption that natural resources are infinite and that technological innovation by itself will encounter all solutions needed.) [2.] Promoting free cultural exchange by abandoning innovation-inhibiting conceptions of pseudo-scarcity in the cultural world (based on the assumption that the free flow of culture must be restricted through excessive patents, copyright, intellectual property, etc.)" https://p2pfoundation.net/the-p2p-foundation/about-the-p2p-foundation [accessed 22 August 2021].
[194] Sowell, 1995, p. 8.
[195] Wilson and Walton, 2019, pp. 16-8.
[196] Rising Up! quoted in Wilson and Walton, 2019, p. 18.
[197] *Ibid.*, p. 19.
[198] Arrow, 2020, pp. 308-16.
[199] Roger Hallam, "The Civil Resistance Model", in Farrell et al., 2019, p. 104.
[200] Hallam's estimate draws from Erica Chenoweth and Maria J. Stephan, *Why Civil Resistance Works: The Strategic Logic of Nonviolent Conflict* by Columbia University Press, 2012 ("3.5%" in their estimate). Ronan McNern, "One by One: A Media Strategy", in Farrell et al., 2019, p. 126.

[201] Roger Hallam, "The Civil Resistance Model", in Farrell et al., 2019, p. 99.
[202] Wilson and Walton, 2019, p. 30.
[203] "The Extinction Rebellion Guide to Citizens' Assemblies", Extinction Rebellion, 25 June 2019.
[204] Wilson and Walton, 2019, pp. 31–5.
[205] Roger Hallam, "The Civil Resistance Model", in Farrell et al., 2019, p. 102.
[206] See Ronan McNern, "One by One: A Media Strategy", in Farrell et al., 2019, pp. 126–30.
[207] Vault, London, 22 February 2020, filmed.
[208] Miles Glyn and Clare Farrell, "Arts Factory", in Farrell et al., 2019, p. 121.
[209] https://www.nokillmag.com/articles/xr-youth-interview [accessed 15 August 2021].
[210] *Ibid.*
[211] https://www.aston.ac.uk/latest-news/extinction-rebellions-activists-more-likely-be-new-protesting-study-shows [accessed 26 August 2021].
[212] https://capitalresearch.org/article/unabombers-without-bombs-part-1/ [accessed 15 August 2021].
[213] https://www.telegraph.co.uk/environment/2019/09/06/getty-heiress-donates-500000-fund-backs-extinction-rebellion/ [accessed 15 August 2021].
[214] https://web.archive.org/web/20191019174849/https://www.telegraph.co.uk/news/2019/10/10/extinction-rebellion-funded-charity-set-one-britains-richest/ [accessed 15 August 2021].
[215] Wilson and Walton, 2019, pp. 56–7.
[216] "20,000 to 40,000" pounds or euros. *Ibid.*, p. 57.
[217] *Ibid.*, p. 58.
[218] Etzioni-Halevy, 1993, p. 204.
[219] "At times it is the [central] Power which aligns with the periphery as a means to strengthen itself and weaken the subsidiary power centres; at other times, it is the subsidiary power centres which engage with the periphery to undermine and overtake the primary Power. Whatever section is aligning with this periphery, it should be noted that without this alliance between a power centre and the periphery, the periphery itself is basically irrelevant. Without the assistance of a centre of power, any action by the periphery is, by virtue of lacking institutional embodiment and political protection, at best sporadic and ineffective. A popular protest, rebellion, or any other form of dissenting action by the periphery, if it has no support from an element in the power structure, will quickly fade into irrelevance; if it does have this support, it will find itself supplied with resources, exposure, protection, and institutional embodiment", C.A. Bond, *Nemesis: The Jouvenalian vs. The Liberal Model of Human Orders*, Imperium Press, 2019.

[220] Including Maria Balshaw, Director of Tate: https://www.standard.co.uk/news/londoners-diary/londoners-xr-tate-boss-maria-balshaw-b956860.html [accessed 24 September 2021].
[221] See the Paris Treaty, COP26, G7 statements and briefing documents for internal and public consumption.
[222] Email from "Insider B" to AA, 9 September 2021.
[223] See https://www.bournbrookmag.com/home/museums-deconstructed-by-degrees [accessed 5 October 2021].
[224] Email from "Insider A" to AA, 28 July 2021.
[225] *Ibid.*
[226] *Ibid.*
[227] https://www.restoretrust.org.uk/ [accessed 28 July 2021].
[228] National Trust, *Interim Report on the Connections between Colonialism and Properties now in the Care of the National Trust, Including Links with Historic Slavery*, September 2020.
[229] https://www.dailymail.co.uk/news/article-8923287/National-Trust-chair-praises-BLM-human-rights-movement-no-party-political-affiliations.html [accessed 28 July 2021].
[230] Company no. 252131, Charity no. 313024.
[231] https://esmeefairbairn.org.uk/about-esmee/diversity-equity-and-inclusion/ [accessed 20 August 2021].
[232] https://www.museumsassociation.org/about/ [accessed 20 August 2021].
[233] https://www.museumsassociation.org/events/conference-2021-brave-new-world/programme/?utm_campaign=2014339_Conference%202021%20campaign%203%20keynotes&utm_medium=email&utm_source=Museums%20Association&dm_i=2VBX,1769V,27LZBM,4N3C3,1 [accessed 6 October 2021].
[234] https://www.museumsassociation.org/campaigns/decolonising-museums/ [accessed 21 August 2021].
[235] Headlines from the MA's email newsletters: "'Opinions are changing': Berlin's new cultural venue tackles colonial legacies", "How can we use technology in a way that is rooted in Blackness?", "Diversity must be at the heart of good governance", "Beyond the black square: Slow progress on sector's anti-racist commitment", "Museums and Black Lives Still Matter".
[236] https://forarthistory.org.uk/about/our-vision/ [accessed 14 September 2021].
[237] https://forarthistory.org.uk/art-history-festival-programme/ [accessed 16 September 2021].
[238] https://icom.museum/en/resources/standards-guidelines/museum-definition/ [accessed 12 October 2021].
[239] https://icom.museum/en/news/icom-announces-the-alternative-museum-definition-that-will-be-subject-to-a-vote/ [accessed 12 October

240 https://www.museumsassociation.org/museums-journal/opinion/2019/10/01102019-definition-just-start-of-conversation/ [accessed 12 October 2021].
241 The ICA lists Birkbeck and Kingston University as research partners: https://ica.art/thanks [accessed 3 September 2021].
242 https://www.gold.ac.uk/news/10-years-of-forensic-architecture/ [accessed 14 August 2021].
243 Kabir Jhala, "Manchester gallery accused of provoking racial discord over exhibition on environmental effects of Israel-Palestine conflict", *The Art Newspaper*, 12 August 2021 [accessed 14 August 2021].
244 Quoted in Jhala, 2021.
245 https://www.gold.ac.uk/news/10-years-of-forensic-architecture/ [accessed 14 August 2021].
246 *Ibid.*
247 "[FA] have closed the exhibition at Whitworth Art Gallery after Manchester University removed a statement from the show declaring that the activist authors of the work were supportive of Palestinians", *The Jackdaw*, no. 159, September/October 2021, p. 23.
248 See Alexander Adams, "The best of British junk", *Standpoint*, Issue 112, June 2019, p. 69.
249 London attendance figures of Turner Prize display "flatlined" in the preceding decade. Declan Long and Laura Gascoigne, "Is the Turner Prize still relevant at 30?", *Apollo*, November 2014.
250 Sholette, 2017, pp. 131–2.
251 https://web.archive.org/web/20210528191712/https://www.tate.org.uk/art/art-terms/s/socially-engaged-practice [accessed 10 August 2021].
252 *Ibid.*
253 http://www.arraystudiosbelfast.com/array-collective.html [accessed 13 May 2021].
254 http://www.cooking-sections.com/info [accessed 13 May 2021].
255 http://gentleradical.org/what/ [accessed 13 May 2021].
256 https://projectartworks.org/the-organisation/ [accessed 13 May 2021].
257 "Turner Prize–Nominated Collective Criticizes Tate's 'Exploitative Practices'", *ArtForum*, 11 May 2021 [accessed 13 May 2021].
258 *Ibid.*
259 For a prediction of this, see Adams, 2019, p. 47.
260 Billy Childish and Charles Thomson, "The Stuckist Manifesto", 1999, in Danchev, 2011, pp. 425–9.
261 *Ibid.*
262 For discussion of paraphrasing and plagiarising by YBAs, see Julian Stallabrass, *High Art Lite*, Verso, 2001, and esp. Charles Thomson, "The Art

Damien Hirst Stole", *The Jackdaw*, no. 93, September/October 2010, pp. 10–2, Charles Thomson, "The Art Damien Hirst Stole, Part II", *The Jackdaw*, no. 94, November/December 2010, pp. 18–9.
263 Email from CT to AA, 6 August 2021.
264 Email from EG to AA, 7 August 2021.
265 Richard Bledsoe, "Reclaiming Art as a Force for Liberty", 11 June 2021, https://www.americanthinker.com/articles/2021/06/reclaiming_art_as_a_force_for_liberty.html [accessed 10 August 2021].
266 Sir Nicholas Serota, Director of the Tate Gallery (1988–2017) and Chair of ACE (2017–).
267 Email from ELS to AA, 13 August 2021.
268 https://uncw.edu/arts/artivism/ [accessed 19 August 2021].
269 https://informal.utexas.edu/classes/introduction-artivism-art-activism [accessed 19 August 2021].
270 https://sites.utexas.edu/queerandtransvoices/2021/07/the-power-of-artivism-an-interview-with-julio-salgado/ [accessed 19 August 2021].
271 https://diversity.wisc.edu/tag/artivism-student-action-program/ [accessed 19 August 2021].
272 https://www.adelphi.edu/artivism/ [accessed 1 August 2021].
273 *Ibid.*
274 Helguera, 2011, p. 4.
275 https://www.ljmu.ac.uk/research/centres-and-institutes/the-centre-for-the-study-of-crime-criminalisation-and-social-exclusion/research-and-expertise/artivism [accessed 19 August 2021].
276 Richard H. Thaler and Cass R. Sunstein, *Nudge: The Final Edition*, Yale, 2021.
277 All CAA data from https://www.c4aa.org [accessed 2 August 2021].
278 "The Yes Lab is a series of brainstorms and trainings to help activist groups carry out media-getting creative actions, focused on their own campaign goals", https://theyesmen.org/lab [accessed 2 August 2021].
279 "Intelligent Mischief is a creative studio and futures design lab unleashing Black imagination to shape the future. We create spaces where Black folks can collectively imagine beautiful futures together. […] We are building a global archipelago of Black utopias, liberated zones where Black people are thriving, joyful, sovereign and free; a network of maroon societies and liberated zones, dreamed of and constructed by Black folks, practicing Afro-indigenous ways of being, resting, thriving, living joyful, sovereign, expansive and interdependent lives free from the systems that have harmed us for centuries", https://www.intelligentmischief.com/about [accessed 2 August 2021].
280 Beautiful Trouble "believe in people power and the game-changing role that creativity, humor, joy, and mischief can play in the struggle for a

better world. We practice shared leadership, modified consensus-based decision making, anti-oppression politics, and international and intersectional solidarity", https://www.beautifultrouble.org/about [accessed 2 August 2021].

[281] Poch and Poch, 2018, p. 9.
[282] Sholette, 2017, p. 198.
[283] https://www.collectivelyfree.org/artivism/ [accessed 19 August 2021].
[284] Arte Util redefines aesthetics as social action: "Re-establish aesthetics as a system of transformation", https://www.arte-util.org/open-call/ [accessed 1 September 2021].
[285] Lucy Lippard, "The More Things Change…", in Reilly, 2018, p. 7.
[286] Whitney Chadwick, *Women, Art, and Society*, Thames & Hudson, 2012, p. 344.
[287] Press release, 2 August 2021.
[288] https://artforjusticefund.org/ [accessed 23 August 2021].
[289] https://www.phf.org.uk/ [accessed 20 May 2020].
[290] https://www.freelandsfoundation.co.uk/documents/freelands_foundation_annual_report_2017.pdf 2017 [accounts accessed 20 May 2020].
[291] https://www.afiniti.com/team/elisabeth-murdoch/ [accessed 20 May 2020].
[292] https://outset.org.uk/ [accessed 20 May 2020].
[293] Hudson, 2019.
[294] https://visitmima.com/whats-on/single/project-space-1-the-office-of-useful-art/ [accessed 1 September 2021].
[295] https://www.arte-util.org/about/colophon/ [accessed 20 May 2020].
[296] Stephanie Bertrand, "Useful Curating", 2020, http://ormstonhouse.com/wp-content/uploads/2019/09/tsp_useful-curating_final.pdf [accessed 20 May 2020].
[297] Source: MIMA website [accessed 1 September 2021].
[298] See Alexander Adams, "Institutional Support for the Iconoclasm of 2020", in *Toppling Statues*, PSSA, 2021, pp. 141–51.
[299] See Adams, 2019, p. 122.
[300] M.K. Asante, 2008, quoted in Korpe, 2013, p. 3.
[301] Benjamin Barson and Gizelxanath Rodriguez, "Artivism and decolonization: A brief theory history and practice of cultural production as political activism", 5 September 2019, https://nmbx.newmusicusa.org/artivism-and-decolonization-a-brief-theory-history-and-practice-of-cultural-production-as-political-activism/ [accessed 1 August 2021].
[302] For a framing of progressives as outsiders in terms of institutional power, see Grant H. Kester, "Ongoing Negotiations", in Kester, 1998, pp. 1–19.
[303] Morgan Quaintance, "Looking Back in Anger: Ten Years On", *Art Monthly*, no. 442, December 2020/January 2021, p. 7.

[304] https://www.lib.uchicago.edu/collex/exhibits/artivism-italy-and-social-justice/ [accessed 1 August 2021].
[305] Bernárdez Rodal, 2019, p. 26.
[306] *Ibid.*; Delaure and Fink, 2017, pp. 10–1.
[307] Poet in the City is a London based organisation, supported by ACE. "Poet in the City helps people and places tell their stories, creates access to challenging ideas, attracts radically new audiences, brings about social and behavioural change, and creates awe-inspiring large-scale entertainment", https://www.poetinthecity.co.uk/about-us [accessed 17 August 2021].
[308] Poet in the City, press release, 16 August 2021.
[309] *Manifesto for Artists*, Design and Artists Copyright Society, 2021, p. 30.
[310] See Abbing, 2014, and Sholette, 2017, pp. 54–7.
[311] See Abbing, 2014.
[312] Martha Rosler, "Theses on Defunding", 1982, in Kester, 1998, pp. 94–102.
[313] Withdrawal of NEA funding is "pauperization of artists". Compare this to arguments about welfare cuts. Martha Rosler, "Theses on Defunding", 1982, in Kester, 1998, p. 100.
[314] *Ibid.*, p. 97.
[315] "The current generation of artists sees art as a system and knows how to operate by its rules", *ibid.*, p. 98.
[316] Helguera, 2011, p. 63.
[317] Coco Fusco, "Fantasies of Oppositionality", 1988, in Kester, 1998, p. 61.
[318] ICA press release, 16 November 2020.
[319] https://www.artnews.com/art-news/news/latinx-artist-fellowship-2021-1234598335/ [accessed 13 August 2021].
[320] Abbing, 2014.
[321] https://www.dacs.org.uk/latest-news/artist-salary-research?category=For+Artists&title=N [accessed 26 July 2021].
[322] TBR, *Livelihoods of Visual Artists: 2016 Data Report*, Arts Council, 2016, pp. 1–2.
[323] Abbing, 2014, p. 112.
[324] Grant H. Kester, "Alternative Arts Sector and the Imaginary Public", in Kester, 1998, p. 130.
[325] www.lauragodfreyisaacs.com [accessed 26 July 2021].
[326] Contrast this with Korpe's assessment of Arab artivism: "Artivism becomes something quite different in places where people have the choice to become artivists, can afford material, have networks of support and even get credited for their work in magazines or add it to their Curriculum Vitae's [sic]", Korpe, 2013, p. 51.
[327] https://www.theguardian.com/artanddesign/2018/jan/31/manchester-art-gallery-removes-waterhouse-naked-nymphs-painting-prompt-conversation?CMP=fb_gu [accessed 1 February 2018].

328 Interview with Andrew Doyle, YouTube, 28 January 2021, https://www.youtube.com/watch?v=bIrgJEJn97s
329 See Adams, 2020, pp. 83–100.
330 Krause, 2011, p. 11.
331 Ibid., p. 15.
332 Ibid., p. 18. For a contrary call to occupy mainstream institutions, see Trend, "Cultural Struggle and Educational Activism", in Kester, 1998, p. 170.
333 Krause, 2011, p. 89.
334 Ibid., p. 93.
335 For more artivist opposition to aesthetics, see Coco Fusco, "Fantasies of Oppositionality", 1988, in Kester, 1998, pp. 66–7.
336 Thompson, 2015, p. 111.
337 Witness the hostility of BLM and Antifa (both organisations putatively supporting minority-ethnic groups) towards (respectively) black evangelical Christians and conservative ethnic-Asian journalists.
338 Heartney and Posner, 2013, p. 192.
339 Ibid., p. 191.
340 https://hyperallergic.com/682889/tania-bruguera-agreed-to-leave-cuba-in-exchange-for-release-of-25-prisoners/?utm_medium=email&utm_campaign=D101121&utm_content=D101121+CID_cda03fe18e2d0de73ae762ab62b460d3&utm_source=hn&utm_term=Tania%20Bruguera%20Agreed%20to%20Leave%20Cuba%20in%20Exchange%20for%20Release%20of%2025%20Prisoners [accessed 11 October 2021].
341 https://carmenemanuelapopa.com/news_content.php?t=Design%20For%20Social%20Innovation [accessed 19 August 2021].
342 http://b1-akt.com/ [accessed 19 August 2021].
343 http://b1-akt.com/who-we-work-with [accessed 19 August 2021].
344 "*Humans for Women est une association étudiante féministe intersectionnelle*", http://www.humansforwomen.org/ [accessed 19 August 2021].
345 https://eca.unwomen.org/en/digital-library/multimedia/2021/06/mural-artivism [accessed 19 August 2021].
346 https://www.atlanticcouncil.org/commentary/photo-essays/how-artivism-can-change-society-in-afghanistan-and-beyond/ [accessed 2 August 2021].
347 https://www.stripes.com/news/george-floyd-mural-painted-near-kabuls-green-zone-1.633812 [accessed 19 August 2021].
348 For socially conscious art of the mid-twentieth century see Christine Lindey, *Art for All: British Socially Committed Art from the 1930s to the Cold War*, Artery Publications, 2018, etc.
349 In 2019, a survey of British people found that 44% want immigration reduced, 39% want immigration to remain as it is, 17% want it increased:

https://migrationobservatory.ox.ac.uk/resources/briefings/uk-public-opinion-toward-immigration-overall-attitudes-and-level-of-concern/ [accessed 1 September 2021].
350 Adams, 2020, pp. 104–5.
351 United Nations, 2010.
352 Burnham, 2014, p. 219.
353 See Sowell, 1995.
354 Reilly, 2018, pp. 220–1.
355 Whitney Chadwick and Isabelle de Courtivron (eds.), *Significant Others: Creativity & Intimate Partnership*, Thames & Hudson, 1993, p. 10.
356 Helguera, 2011, p. 4.
357 David Thorne, quoted in Sholette, 2017, p. 168.
358 Hannah Black, interview, *Art Monthly*, no. 441, November 2020, p. 5.
359 "Turner Prize–Nominated Collective Criticizes Tate's 'Exploitative Practices'", *ArtForum*, 11 May 2021 [accessed 13 May 2021].
360 Michelle Williams Gamaker, "On Fictional Activism", in Deepwell, 2020, p. 41.
361 https://unitedwedream.org/heretostay/summer-of-dreams/ [accessed 20 August 2021].
362 https://egyptianstreets.com/ [accessed 20 August 2021].
363 https://egyptianstreets.com/egyptianstreets/ [accessed 20 August 2021].
364 Korpe, 2013.
365 Helguera, 2011, p. 18.
366 Facebook account Turning Tables Tunisia, active until 2014.
367 https://www.egyptindependent.com/ongoing-demonization-egyptian-metalheads/ [accessed 3 September 2021].
368 Mark Levine, "Putting the 'Jamming' into Culture Jamming", in Delaure and Fink, 2017, p. 125.
369 Pahwa and Winegar, 2012.
370 Korpe, 2013, p. 50.
371 Quoted in https://www.iemed.org/publication/from-activism-to-artivism-new-forms-of-youth-activism-in-the-aftermath-of-the-20-february-movement/ [accessed 19 August 2021].
372 https://www.iemed.org/publication/from-activism-to-artivism-new-forms-of-youth-activism-in-the-aftermath-of-the-20-february-movement/#_ftn8 [accessed 19 August 2021].
373 See Ahmed Bensaada, *Arabesque$: Enquête sur le rôle des Etats-Unis dans les révoltes arabes*, Investig'Action, 2015.
374 Arrow, 2020, p. 247.
375 *Ibid.*, p. 248.
376 *Ibid.*, pp. 249–50.
377 Covert CIA backing for avant-garde publications and cultural events

available to foreign nations is amply documented. See https://www.thenation.com/article/archive/when-cia-was-nea/ [accessed 22 August 2021].
378 Abbing, 2014.
379 Cildo Meireles's 1971 performance. Helguera, 2011, p. 65.
380 This position has already been dismissed by one artivist supporter: "Conservatives claim to be defending the interests of 'taxpayers,' whose hard-earned income is being expropriated by the state to fund the perversions of a depraved minority under the guise of 'art'" (Grant H. Kester, "Alternative Arts Sector and the Imaginary Public", in Kester, 1998, p. 103). Many conservatives agree but would be puzzled by the scare quotes around the word "taxpayers", as if such beings were merely putative.
381 *Ibid.*, p. 118.
382 Burnham, 2020, p. 205.
383 https://frieze.com/article/chelsea-manning-make-first-public-uk-appearance-londons-ica [accessed 2 October 2018].
384 "The objects for which the Company is established are to promote the education of the community by encouraging the understanding, appreciation and development of the arts generally and particularly of contemporary art as expressed in painting, etching, engraving, drawing, poetry, philosophy, literature, drama, music, opera, ballet, sculpture, architecture, designs, photography, films, radio and television of educational and cultural value" (Article 3(i), Memorandum of Association, 22 July 1947, after amendment).
385 Section 1.1, Campaigning and political activity guidance for Charities, Charity Commission, 1 March 2008, https://www.gov.uk/government/publications/speaking-out-guidance-on-campaigning-and-political-activity-by-charities-cc9/speaking-out-guidance-on-campaigning-and-political-activity-by-charities.
386 Since 2013 the ICA has averaged a million a year from the Arts Council of England—£1,025,147 this year, plus £93,940 from the Heritage Lottery. In 2010 it received a special £1.2 million bail-out in order to rescue it from insolvency. The Arts Council of England is described variously in the ICA's annual accounts as "principal funder" and "principal supporter".
387 Alexander Adams, "ICA, Artivism and Illegality", *The Jackdaw*, no. 152, July/August 2020, p. 43.
388 ICA press release, 10 April 2020, https://www.ica.art/digital/ica-daily [accessed 20 July 2021].
389 *Ibid.*, 29 April 2020.
390 *Ibid.*, 30 April 2020.
391 *Ibid.*, 5 May 2020.
392 *Ibid.*, 7 May 2020.

[393] *Ibid.*, 30 May 2020.
[394] *Ibid.*, 2 June 2020.
[395] *Ibid.*, 3 June 2020.
[396] *Ibid.*, 4 June 2020.
[397] *Ibid.*, 12 April 2020.
[398] *Ibid.*, 21 May 2020.
[399] *Ibid.*, 26 May 2020.
[400] *Ibid.*, 15 May 2020.
[401] *Ibid.*, 29 April 2020.
[402] *Ibid.*, 17 November 2020.
[403] *Ibid.*, 1 May 2020.
[404] *Ibid.*, 9 May 2020.
[405] *Ibid.*, 12 April 2020.
[406] *Ibid.*, 20 November 2020.
[407] *Ibid.*, 2 June 2020.
[408] *Ibid.*, 3 June 2020.
[409] *Ibid.*, 1 June 2020.
[410] *Ibid.*, 3 June 2020.
[411] *Ibid.*, 9 November 2020.
[412] *Ibid.*, 24 May 2020.
[413] *Ibid.*, 6 May 2020.
[414] *Ibid.*, 5 April 2020.
[415] *Ibid.*, 28 March 2020.
[416] *Ibid.*, 30 May 2020.
[417] *Ibid.*, 10 April 2020.
[418] *Ibid.*, 11 April 2020.
[419] *Ibid.*, 9 November 2020.
[420] *Ibid.*, 12 November 2020.
[421] *Ibid.*, 4 April 2020.
[422] *Ibid.*, 9 April 2020.
[423] *Ibid.*, 5 April 2020.
[424] *Ibid.*, 29 April 2020.
[425] *Ibid.*, 9 May 2020.
[426] *Ibid.*, 9 April 2020.
[427] *Ibid.*, 30 April 2020.
[428] *Ibid.*, 24 May 2020.
[429] *Ibid.*, 10 November 2020.
[430] *Ibid.*, 30 April 2020.
[431] First published in *The Jackdaw*, no. 159, September/October 2021, pp. 10–1.
[432] Helen Stephenson CBE, Chief Executive Officer of CCE.
[433] https://ica.art/exhibitions/war-inna-babylon [accessed 30 June 2021].
[434] "This exhibition is part of an ICA programme dedicated to racial justice,

social justice and liveable futures for all [...]", *ibid*.

[435] "The objects for which the Company is established are to promote the education of the community by encouraging the understanding, appreciation and development of the arts generally and particularly of contemporary art as expressed in painting, etching, engraving, drawing, poetry, philosophy, literature, drama, music, opera, ballet, sculpture, architecture, designs, photography, films, radio and television of educational and cultural value" (Article 3(i), Memorandum of Association, 22 July 1947, after amendment).

[436] Section 1.1, Campaigning and political activity guidance for Charities, Charity Commission, 1 March 2008, https://www.gov.uk/government/publications/speaking-out-guidance-on-campaigning-and-political-activity-by-charities-cc9/speaking-out-guidance-on-campaigning-and-political-activity-by-charities [accessed 30 June 2021].

www.ingramcontent.com/pod-product-compliance
Lightning Source LLC
Chambersburg PA
CBHW071532220526
45469CB00003B/739